'I will take you through the Stars'
By The Traveller

Goliath Publishing

First Published in Great Britain in 2013
Goliath Publishing

USA Edition printed by CreateSpace 2013

This edition first published in 2013

This book is a work of non-fiction based on the life, experiences and recollections of
The Traveller. In many cases the names, places, dates or detail may have been changed
to protect the privacy of others.

ISBN 978 0 9558418 1 1

Typeset 12 /14 / 18pt Garamond / Times New Roman
Printed and bound in Great Britain by Goliath Publishing

www.goliathpublishing.co.uk
www.goliathpublishing.com

Front Cover

Painting by Dick Twinney on 28 December 2001. Painting based on a vision seen by 'The Traveller' 14 September 2001 of the World Trade Centre disaster 11 September 2001.

"I saw golden strands of light over the debris in the New York World Trade Centre and figures being lifted, rising up. All of this was being watched over by one beautiful light being - an angel. The angel was glowing with golden and white light and I sensed the feeling of peace and stillness as I heard, **'Religion, colour or country makes no difference all are the same, all are one, one with God.'**

The Traveller

***

Contents

Introduction

This book is an autobiographical account of a remarkable ladies witness to often frightening revelations about the misuse of power, particularly within the Catholic Church. Signed letters, photos and other evidence mentioned herein have been retained as proof of this witness of account.

While I know every priest or nun cannot be tarnished with the same brush it is evident that after reading this gripping book anyone who may consider themselves religious in any way or form may well have to revaluate and soul search as to just what that is and means to them.

The author's name has been changed to 'The Traveller' throughout this book to protect her identity and well-being, as have the names of other people been changed for similar reasons.

(Editor)

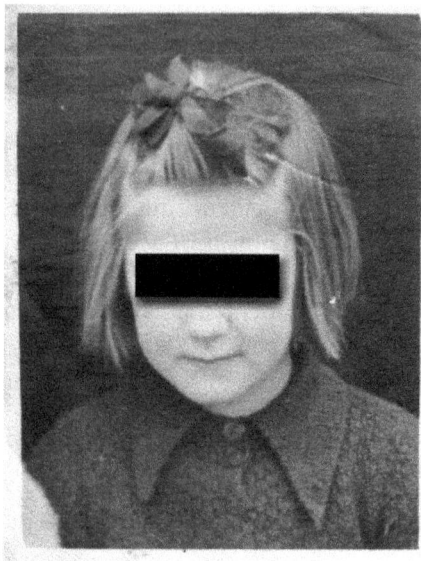

Chapter 1

The Early Years

I was born The Traveller₁ and originated from Ireland.
The following true story is about my life. This true story starts from the age I can first remember things - as a child.

When I went to call for my friend to play I would '*see*'₂ some houses with a lot of black smoke inside. I was afraid to go in. I would stand at the door, and then I would '*see*' a row going on with fighting and shouting that had happened days before. But of course I could never understand all of this.

As children we also went around swapping comics and I would see scenes of the father or mammy hitting the children. It upset me very much and when I was at Mass (church) I could *hear*₃ people talking and they would be sitting seven or eight seats in front of me, whispering as the priest said the Mass. At times I would '*see*' a figure of a beautiful light standing beside the priest.

I would ask my friend if she could see anything beside the priest. I would hear a voice say 'she can't *see*'. They could never '*see*' anything.

One friend would laugh and say I was a 'queer old thing'. I was afraid to tell people as my mam had told me not to say any of this to anyone as they would not understand.

Then one day, while in the house on my own, a man came in. My mam had just gone to the neighbour's house. He talked for a while, and then he undid his trousers. He took out his penis and started to tell me what he wanted to do.

I had no idea what he was talking about. Above and in front of me, like images on a big screen, I was shown what he wanted me to do. Then I heard a voice saying, '*get out of the house – now!*' I was stuck to the floor. I remember looking around to see who was talking to me. I even looked to the ceiling but could not see anyone. As the man came closer to me I saw a figure like white smoke go all around me. I felt it quickly and with that I was out of the door and on the street.

I was so frightened and confused. I didn't know what to do. I had never seen a man's penis before. When my brother would get undressed to get into bed my sister and I would put our heads under the blankets 'til he got into bed. Sometimes we would pretend to see him and shout and laugh. He would nearly break his neck jumping into bed. So to see this man doing this frightened me very much.

Outside I remembered he didn't look very nice. He had all this black smoke around him and his body looked terrible. Even his face felt very cold. Then suddenly I felt the white smoke leave me. I saw it about two feet in front of me and then it faded - I felt lost.

I heard a friend shout out my name.

"Come and have a race," Ann said. She lived opposite us. Her house was bigger and they had gardens in the front and the back. At the back of the houses was a lane; we would stand at each end of the lane and race down, passing each other at the bottom and back to the start. We did this for a long time and it helped me.

I was just going to tell my friend what had happened when her brother came and asked us to go to the dump with him to get wheels to make a dilly[4]. So I was with them all day 'till late evening.

Soon it came time to go home. I was so frightened; I felt fear just walking through the hallway to the door. They had a lot of coats hanging just behind the front door and I was afraid to go past them. My friend laughed at me. She stood at the door, while I walked down the street. When I got into my house I wanted to tell my mam about the incident with the stranger, but there were other things going on, so I left it.

The next day I saw the man again. He was angry. He told me not to tell anyone about what had happened or I would get into trouble. He caught me again weeks later and then the abuse started.

I saw my friend Ann and her brother Paddy[5], he had made the dilly. "Come for a ride!" he shouted.

I jumped in behind him as he speed down the main street.

Back in those times there were only two cars that I can remember. One - the hearse and the other - the car the people travelled in behind the hearse - the funeral car. Farmers used to arrive on a horse and cart with potatoes and vegetables.

We were going great guns[6] down the street, when around from the corner came the hearse. Paddy panicked, pulling on the rope to get the dilly to go left. It hit the curb with a thud and we all went head over heels onto the grass verge.

We were afraid to laugh as we stood and watched the hearse go by.

My foot was hurting. Looking at the coffin I saw a great golden light. It left the car and went to stand beside a crying woman. The light seemed to touch the women's head. I asked Paddy "did you see that?"

"What?" he said.

Again I was *'told'* he couldn't *see*.

Now looking at the dilly, we realised the front wheel was broken. (Oh well! - Back to the dump to find another.)

I used to go and get messages for some of the people in the street. At the end of the week I would have 6p, sometimes 3p. When I had to buy tea for some people, after smelling it I had to sink my teeth into the packet or I would carefully open the packet to put some tea leaves into my mouth. I would chew it for a while then spit it out. I used to do this in the house as well. But one day on the way back from the shop I was chewing the tea and up in front of me came a huge picture. The sun was shining and it was really hot. I was looking at a young boy in white clothes in a field. He was laughing and talking to people but picking leaves from trees. They had dark skin. Then the picture faded. I spat the tea out and went running home with the shopping.

When I got home I told my mam what had happened. She tried to stop me talking and told me not to say anything to anyone about it. But this wasn't helping me. I wanted to know what was going on. I didn't understand it.

Back in my childhood we had no radio, TV or electric, just an oil lamp on the table and we had never seen coloured people.

At the bottom of town the farmers would bring in their cows to sell. I remember seeing colours around the animals. If a man hit a cow I knew the cow felt it. Its body changed somehow. I also knew when people were telling the truth or not and knew if the person was a good person or not.

Then one day I came home to hear my granny had died. It felt as if someone had cut me with a knife. We went to her house, the room was full of people, yet the place looked dark. I remembered it always being light. Everyone was talking. On the day of the funeral I was standing at the door going into the kitchen, yet looking at the box by the window, where my granny was lying. I saw a big round light come from the window and go by her head. I heard her calling my name. As I walked towards the box a women caught me and told me to go into the kitchen. I could see my mam crying. She was so upset! There was a women talking to her. Standing in the kitchen, I could still see the light around her head, up above the coffin. Then I remembered standing beside her seeing and feeling this lovely light[7].

I never remember her telling me she loved me or giving me a hug, but I could feel it. I knew she did, just standing beside her; the love and warmth just flowed from her.

Back in those days *a child was to be seen and not heard*.

I could hear granny calling me again, as I walked towards the coffin the light was still by her head and then over her hair. I felt such a warm feeling, as if she was still alive. The house looked lit up with light. Next thing a woman had me up in the air telling me to go back from there. I looked back towards the coffin but the light had gone.

I never went back to the house much after that. It never felt the same again.

One day at school I asked a nun if I could talk to her. I told her what had happened with my granny. She asked me where I see and hear all this from. I told her everywhere, in the church, house, school and backyard. I never know when it's going to happen - it just happens. She told me, "it's the devil" and because I was left-handed I would have to write with my right hand. She also told me, "You have to pray more."

I said, "I do pray a lot."

"Well," she said, "you will pray more. You will stay back after school and pray for one hour." She took me to the head nun's office. She told me to kneel in front of the cross on the wall and pray until she came back for me. I seemed to be kneeling for ages. My knees were sore.

The door opened and in she came and told me to go to the chapel and light a candle, get a bottle of holy water and when I had finished praying to go home and throw the holy water all around the house, in my bed and by the doors.

I was told to do all this until she talked to me again. I did this for weeks and in the meantime at school she would make me write with my right hand. I couldn't do it. When she wasn't looking, I would write with my left hand again. If she caught me she would beat my hand. I broke out in a cold sweat trying to write with my right hand. In the end I had a job to write with either hand. One day she caught me again writing with my left hand and took me to the head nun's office. She beat me with a sally cane on my left hand. Then she asked, "Do you still hear things?"

I said, "Yes I do."

"Are you throwing the holy water around like I told you?"

"Yes," I said.

She told me to put my hand on the desk. As I did she brought the cane down on it. She did this for several minutes. I took my hand away. She was so angry. All around her was *red and black smoke* and it smelt terrible. She told me to put my hand back and she beat me again. Then she told me to kneel in front of the cross again and pray till she came back. As soon as she left I was *'told'* to leave and go home. I said, "I can't someone will see me!" Again I was *'told'* to get up and go. As I got up and opened the door, looking down corridor no one was around, so I ran out of the school.

Next day when she saw me she slapped my face. My friend was with me. It really hurt. My head went to one side and once more I was to see her after school. She did the same again, hitting me with the sally stick. As she brought it up I could hear it whistle. I had to kneel and pray as before, only this time she stayed in the room marking and writing. I was there till after five.

When I got home my mam asked, "What's wrong with your face?" The mark of her hand was still there.

I just said, "She (the nun) hit me." I was afraid to tell my mam I had told the nun things I was seeing and hearing as she had told me not to say anything to anyone. But I thought a nun would know; they were after all working for God.

Next morning my mam came to the school, opened the door and called the nun out and told her about my face. My mam shouted at her in front of everyone. I was sent to my desk.

11

During the day I tried to write with my right hand. I was even trying to do it at home but I couldn't. It didn't feel right.

One day I was so engrossed trying to read and write that the nun caught me with the pencil in my left hand. She would hit me with her ruler on the back of my hands. The veins would rise up and it would take me ages to read. The words would jump around the page. I would cover up the words and do a line at a time and the nun told me not to do that, just read.

Oh was I sorry I ever told her anything. After school she asked me if I could sing. She wanted to put me in the choir singing hymns at mass. I said, "No I can't sing." I didn't want to do it. She took me to the piano and started playing. She told me to sing. I couldn't sing - I was shaking. She got the cane again and told me to put my hand on the piano. Oh, I knew this would hurt just like my hand on the desk. I put my hand on the piano, as she brought the cane down I took my hand away. She was furious; she caught my hand and put it on the piano. She told me if I took it away she would hit me longer. She brought the cane down on my hand. The pain went through my whole body. I felt it, even in my feet, my back my shoulders and head. As she did this she asked me, "are you still seeing and hearing things?"

I told her, "Yes."

Her face went red and horrible. As she brought the stick down she said, "and what's he telling you now then?"

I said he *'told'* me you don't want to be here. She stopped the stick still up above her head. I looked at her. She shouted to me to get out.

I did not go back to class; instead I went to the chapel. I usually sit at the back but this time I went to the front. I wanted him (God) to hear and see me. I was so angry I wanted to kick the seat. As I went to kneel down crying I said, "Did you see what she did to me today, did you see it?" I leaned forward, my head in my hands. With that the whole place lit up. I looked to see where it was coming from. I got the loveliest feeling, as if someone you loved had put his or her arms around you. My hands and head didn't hurt anymore. I felt wonderful! This huge white light lasted for several minutes and felt so warm. Then it began to fade - getting smaller and smaller. It seemed to go through the wall at the front of the church, behind the alter.

Now it began to feel cold. I looked around, there was no light now and it was quite dark. I got up and left.

Next morning at school the head nun called me to her office and asked me about the things I *see* and *hear*. She told me to see a priest at 6pm and that I was to sleep with my hands across my chest at night so that if God comes to call me I will be ready. She showed me what to do and again she told me to keep throwing the holy water around the house and keep praying.

Again I was told to kneel in front of the cross and pray. She stayed at her desk. While I did this I seemed to be there for hours. I had a job to walk, when I got up, my knees felt hard and sore.

6pm came and I was standing at the priest's house knocking at the door.

I heard the voice saying *'you will get no help here'*, I wasn't listening.

The housekeeper opened the door and I went inside.

I thought the priest will know. He came in asked about what the nun had told him. I explained to him it was true. I also told him what happened at the church after Sister A had hit me and told him what I had heard while knocking on his door.

His was silent for a while. Then he said, "Go to the chapel, light a candle and pray. Tomorrow you will meet me at the convent at 6pm."

I did what he said. The next day I went to the convent, ringing the bell. I looked above the door to the statue of Our Lady. The door opened I told the nun I was to see the priest here. She went off. I saw the light. It seemed to come from the ceiling I heard, *'this place is going to be closed down.'*

I shouted, "Shut up! Shut up!"

The nun came and looked around and said follow me. She took me to their chapel. All the nuns were there. The priest came to say mass. I was in-between the nuns. I had never been here before. It felt nice. When the mass was over the nuns and

13

priest told me to go home now and pray. They told me to wash myself but don't touch yourself. I didn't know what they meant.

Then I heard *'The convent is going to close'*. I thought it must be the devil. God wouldn't say that. In the days ahead I still had to kneel in front of the cross and pray.

I remember my friend asking me, "Why are you staying behind after school?"

I told her, "To learn to write with my right hand." I was afraid to tell her the devil was with me or she may not play with me. I was so angry I would kick my brown school case home, taking off the surface of the case. Then my mam would tell me off.

Looking back my childhood was very fearful.

Missionaries would come and tell us all what they were doing for all the poor black children in the poor countries. One I remember had a black doll and he would talk to a packed church telling us to put our hands in our pockets and put money in the boxes that were coming around. The missionaries would shout: "You all have plenty compared to these people, who have nothing." I would be *'told'* they are not speaking the truth.

Over the years lots of missionaries came and went. It was always the same story. They are doing so much for the poor black children and we were to give, give and give.

Some of the missionaries looked very bad with black and red auras around them. Sometimes their body had black and red marks on them. It was like I could see right through them. Then one evening I saw one missionary. He had a nice aura. The colours were lovely - like a rainbow. So after mass I went to see him. I told him what I could hear and see. He told me to see my priest. I said I had. Then he said, "The devil is very cunning you know? He gets to young children."

My heart sank, as the missionary spoke I heard *'I am always with you.'* I told the missionary what I had heard. He got me to kneel down. He said, "Pray, I will bless you."

As I left he told me to see my priest again. Then I felt something pull away from me. I couldn't see anything; I was up in the air looking down on myself talking to the missionary. I could see right through him. I was *'told'* to leave. The colours around the missionary were not there anymore, they had gone and I could just *'see'* a man. I was *'told'* - *'that's all he is a man'*.

As I was walking home I couldn't understand all this. But I knew I wasn't going to see the priests or nuns any more.

I remember at mass on Sundays the priest would call out the names of the people that gave them money. I remember quite clearly being *'told'* – *'this is not right'*. There were a lot of large families and poor families who couldn't afford to give much to the Church. They needed it to feed their families.

My friend from Courtown said on Sundays there was always a row in his house between his mam and dad. His mam wanted ½ a crown to give, but if she gave the money then there wouldn't be much food in the house.

But she couldn't bear hearing all the names being called out and theirs left out.

I was *'told'* in Church one Sunday, *'The Church has a lot to answer for.'* I thought this must be the devil talking.

In the town there were only Catholics and Protestants. The nuns and priests would tell us not to talk or have anything to do with the Protestants. Anyone not Catholic was on the wrong road. I went on hearing and seeing things and I didn't want to go to school. I would pretend I was sick. I would let the cold tap water run over my hands 'till they were white and I'd stay at home. I was feed up kneeling in front of the cross praying. Then one day my mam caught me and sent me to school. The nun saw my hands white and told me to put them on the warm pipes. I did but my fingers felt like pins and needles.

Years later my friend and I were out playing. She started to get very bad pains in the side of her stomach and she shouted out. I could see inside her stomach area it was very red and looked to be getting bigger. I was *'told'* to put my hand on her back, as I did this I could feel her pain$_8$. It was bad. We got home and were taken to the doctor. She was taken to the hospital with appendicitis. But I was still having pain and it was getting worse. I too was taken to the hospital. I thought we would be together but I was put in a different hospital. The doctor felt my tummy. I told him where the pain was. He said, "appendicitis, you will need an operation."

Then I heard quite loud, *'there is nothing wrong with you'*. Oh my God I thought, what's going on. I was afraid to tell the doctor what I had heard but a lovely nurse came around and I told her. She laughed, "You will be ok, don't worry."

I had my rosary beads. I told the nurse to leave the beads with me, not to take them away when I have the operation.

Next day the nurse came around. "You were right," she said "you didn't need the operation, your appendix (putting her fingers up) was just this big."

I asked about my friend but she didn't know. I was in a big ward and to my surprise the Protestant girl that lived at the bottom of our street was beside me. I was afraid to talk to her. We looked at each other, but didn't speak. Then I heard, *'I am the same God she is praying to. You are both the same to me.'*

I could not believe it. I was told to talk to her. I started by asking if she had had her appendix out. We talked. After that I found her very nice. We got on quite well, but sadly when we got home we didn't talk again, we just looked at each other as we passed. Yet, I felt great warmth for her.

I also found out my friend was still in hospital. Her appendix had burst and she was very lucky to get to the hospital on time.

I had a black coat, which I always wore. I felt safe in the coat, as I wanted to be covered up. Then when I went to bed I would put the coat on top of the blankets over me. One morning the coat was gone. My mam told me she had burnt it, as it was old and horrible. I felt as if my arm had been cut off. I felt lost. Then I wouldn't go out in the daylight only when it was dark.

When I went to mass I could still hear things. I was often *'told'* they are only going through the motions or they would look at their watches within ten minutes.

My brother, some friends and myself would get a box of fish when the fishermen would come in with their boats. My uncle

16

was on one of the boats. One day we were playing and in front and above of me appeared a huge light. Within the light I could see the boats coming in. I could see the men on the boats and I could even smell the fish. I told my brother, "The boats are in! I'm going down to the harbour."

"No," he said, "they won't be in yet."

But I knew they were. As I was pulling the box of fish up my brother was coming down. So we both carried the box up to the houses. We would sell some and my Mam would have some. When I think back today, we handled all this fish, never washed and then went to school the next day. (*No wonder the nuns told me to wash!*)

One day at school the nun said she wanted to speak to me after class. They had left me alone for a long time. The nun asked me, "Do you still throw the holy water around the house?"

"I still do it," I said.

"And has it stopped? Do you still hear things?"

I was thinking 'do I tell her or not?' I don't want to be kneeling down again. So I said, "I hear sometimes." I wanted to tell her more but I was afraid.

"Right!" she said, "Saturday, come to the convent at 9 o'clock."

I said, "Ok." I thought it would be another mass. Saturday morning came and I was knocking on the convent door. Again looking at the statue of Our Lady, I said, "Help me please!"

The door opened and in I went. It was a huge place. Looking around at the statues I felt something pull away from me. Again I could see myself standing in this hallway and the nun, Sister M, coming for me. As I was looking at myself walking with her she was not looking so nice. Then I heard her tell me I was to get down on my knees and scrub the whole floor on my own. With that the light faded and I was scrubbing the floor. It must have taken me all day. I can't remember much about it. I was just going through the motions of scrubbing. When I finished I had to pray again with the sisters and then Sister Mary showed me out. As I got to the front door I felt this swirl of light go around me. It felt lovely. I remember thinking it can't be the devil, it felt

17

so nice. Then I felt dreadful for thinking that. I was afraid to tell my mam what had happened.

I remember growing up and seeing people coming to my mam to talk and ask her for help, just as they had with gran.

We never knew what it was about. We were always told to go out and play. I remember one priest in particular coming to the house a lot and my mam talking to him. At one time he was telling her to stop. But the people kept coming and my mam would just say, 'The people and children needed a bit of help'. I saw her many times put her dinner or tea to one side to see the people.

One day, a woman called Mrs L from across the road, came to talk to my mam. Again I was told to go out and play. I was bigger now and said, "No, I don't want to go out and play."

I had a slap around the head and was being pushed out of the door.

I heard Mrs L say, "Watch her Nelly, she's going to give you trouble."

With that I heard so loud, *'you will give her no trouble.'*

I didn't like what Mrs L said so when it got dark I went and picked all her lovely daffodils and tulips from her garden and she had the best flower garden of all the people along the row of houses. I used to like looking across from or window at the lovely flowers. I could *'see'* lovely colours around them. Sometimes colours would be 'joined up'.

I came home that night and gave some of the flowers to my mam and friends, some to give to their Mams. Next morning we heard shouting in the street. We looked out the door.

"Oh Mammy of Jesus!" Mrs L was shouting, her hands to her head, looking at her garden. "Who could have done this; I'll feckin swing for them when I find out who did this."

I felt a hand at the back of my neck; my mam was choking me with my jumper. "You did this!" she said, looking at the flowers beside the big oil lamp on the table. She ran out to take the flowers away. "Jesus if she comes over here and sees this lot here!" mam said.

But looking across at the garden the flowers had gone. I knew I had done wrong; the lovely light around the flowers was gone. I was sorry then that I did it. Any time after that if she came to the house I was gone; I didn't have to be told.

In the following years when growing up I learned not to talk to the nuns or priests again about what I was seeing or hearing. I always got hit for it or told to stand outside the door for hours. I remember telling a friend once about it but she laughed at me and said, "I knew you were queer!"

I never told anyone again. But the visions and messages still kept coming. I would ignore them but they still frightened me. I would pray more. I used to talk to God a lot and told him everything. I remember thinking I wish I had listened to my mam for when I had told her about the visions and voices she told me to keep quiet about it and tell no one. I wondered if she and granny had gone through the same thing too.

Then I was nearly fourteen and that meant time to leave school.

The week before I left the nun, Sister M, asked to see my mam. I was worried what she wanted to talk to my mam about.

Next day my mam and I came to see the nun. She was sitting in her office with a big smile on her face. She told us to come in and told my mam "The Traveller is a great girl with her hands for needlework; she has done anything we give her, even button holes."

I remember one day at school the nun told me to go around the classes showing my work. When I got to my sister and her friend Amelle they told me to "Feck off!" with big smiles on their faces. I was afraid to laugh in case the nun saw me.

Then I heard the nun say to my mam, "Would you let her work with Mrs Wright in the town, sewing all the Church and priest garments? That would mean all the altar runners as well."

My mam jumped up, she was so mad. "She is not going to sew your things! Get someone else to do it."

I was delighted as I looked at the nun with her mouth open in surprise at my mam's reaction. My mammy pulled me by the hand out of the office.

19

I left school – (thank God!) I thought.

Notes

The photograph at the beginning of the chapter is of The Traveller and her first day at school.

> 1.   *'The Traveller' is a name that has been made up for the purpose of protecting the identity of the writer, whom has been threatened on more than one occasion.*
> 2.   *The Traveller sees auras and when black or very dark colours are seen this is not a good sign.*
> 3.   Hearing as in spiritual hearing, not everyone hears the things that The Traveller hears or sees as they are at a different vibrational rate.
> 4.   A dilly is a homemade go-cart.
> 5.   Name changed.
> 6.   'Great guns' in this context means 'very fast'.
> 7.   Today I know that if a person is very spiritual they have this light in and around their bodies and still today I can see and feel it.
> 8.   I know now I had helped her and it was her pain I had felt and not mine.

Chapter 2
Working for a Living

I had finished a few jobs then I got a job working at the pottery. The St Vincent's man had come to the door and told me to start work. They got me a job.

At that time my auntie and uncle came home from England. They asked me if I wanted to go back to England with them. My brother didn't want to go but I did.

I had been working in the pottery every Friday. On payday I would buy three-penny bars of chocolate for us all. Dad would buy the six-penny bars for us all.

Then it came to the weekend that my auntie and uncle were going back home. It was time for me to go also. When the time came I didn't want to leave but I felt I had to. I was still afraid of the abuse, although it had stopped for a long time now the man was still around. I was still seeing and hearing things.

21

I thought over in England all would be fine and I would stay away from the Protestants. I left Ireland for the first time in my life, as a little child, still in my white ankle socks. I was so excited about the trip!

I arrived at Brighton, got to their house and met my cousins for the first time. The house looked lovely. They had everything and their friends would come around on Saturday and sit around for toast and tea or lemonade and talk. It was lovely.

My uncle got me a job in the factory he worked at. First in the office doing figures and making up overtime hours. I was working with an elderly man. He was very good to me, showing me what to do. The workers would come up to me for their wages that I would hand out.

One girl, Brenda, I got to like very much. She asked me to come and work beside her soldering electrical equipment. I asked if I could change my job and I did.

Brenda and I got on so well. I felt as if I had known her all my life. I remember asking her if she was catholic. She laughed right out. "No, I am not," she said, "I don't go to any church."

I remember the priest saying "Pagan England" but I liked Brenda and I was going to stay friends with her. She had lovely colours around her with lots of pinks.

I asked my auntie where the church was. "Oh, it's a long way off. You would have to catch a bus. I will write it out for you and where to get off. Just give it to the driver."

With that I was *'told'* - *'you will know where to get off.'* (Oh, I thought, not again. Not all the way over here. Oh God I thought, please don't let it happen here!) Well Saturday came and I got on the bus for the first time on my own to the town (my auntie lived just outside). I had my piece of paper she had written where to get off. As the bus was stopping near a park I was *"told"* - *get off here!* I did this. The bus conductor said, "You need the next stop!"

"It's ok." I said, "I'll walk in the park first, thank you."

I got off and made my way into the park, it was lovely, it had a big tree with a white base around it and lots of flowers. As I stopped to look around it happened again. I saw it as a big dance hall with men in uniform and women with huge big long dresses, all dancing. The men were in blue jackets and trousers with a light strip down the side. It looked as if swords were on their side.

I had never seen anything like it before. Next minute I was back in the park again. It frightened me. (What's happening to me I thought?)

I sat for a few minutes looking at the flowers and then I went to the shops. I asked for a ¼ of Irish Roses. The man looked at me.

I thought: (this is the first time I had money to buy Irish Roses).

The man said, "We don't have Irish Roses'.

Looking around at all the sweet jars he took down a big glass jar (they were Irish roses). "We only have these chocolates," he said.

I felt stupid; I couldn't say that's them. "No," I said, "they are not the ones. I'll have the ¼ of bull's eyes instead." He knew these.

I walked around the shops and went back to my aunties. I was afraid to tell her what had happened.

"Did you see the church?" she asked.

"Yes. I'll go there another time." But I hadn't seen the church. The whole experience had thrown me of track altogether.

"We'll have to get you new clothes," she said, "and some stockings and shoes." That's another story!

I went back to Ireland for a holiday to see my family. I was so home sick. We went to the pictures one night with my sister and met a lovely fella. I felt as if I knew him, yet I had never met him before. He kept throwing rolled up balls of paper at us. Outside we got talking and he asked me to go out with him. I said, "Yes."

We made a date. My sister was talking to her friends as I walked over to them. I found out the boys we had been talking with had been farmers from the country and I should not go out with them as they would get into trouble fighting. There were three brothers and they would come in around Gorey₁ in a red car looking for girls. This didn't bother me. The colours around them were good. So I went by that. I didn't go back to England. Instead I went with Paddy. We got on so well. I stayed in Gorey. Then he asked me to marry him. We got married July 1963. It was lovely. I felt so happy and he told me he was happy too. But as we set off for Dublin and our honeymoon and the first night came I was so scared. I couldn't do it. As much as I tried to control it, the fear was getting worse.

He was great, "don't worry," he said. So we sat and talked all night. Next night the same, I cried so much and I couldn't tell him what was wrong.

Then months later he said, "We'll go to England with my brother and get work. Maybe we'll be better there."

He went first and got us a place to stay. When I arrived in Croydon the place was so different with so many people and so much going on. I loved jumping on the buses. There were none in Gorey. I made friends with the girl that lived beside us. She was from Northern Ireland. She wanted a job and asked me if I would go with her to the interview. "Yes," I said.

As we walked to the factory there were boards in all the windows with writing on them saying, 'No blacks! No Irish! No dogs!' I said to Mary, "Why do they do that? What's wrong with us?" Anyone coming over from Ireland would only get a place to live with Irish landladies or sometimes Indian people would take the Irish, if they didn't drink.

I was told there were lots of black people living here. I had never seen a black person. In Ireland, there were only Catholics and Protestants.

In the factory we saw the forewoman; she was also Irish and asked me if I would like a job.

"Oh yes, I would."

She told us to come back on Monday. I got home telling Paddy all about it. We walked together to work. We got on so well together. But at home – still no sex!

At the factory we were put on different jobs. Mary went one way and I the other. The forewoman took me to a big table. There was a big trolley, full with hot water bottles. She gave me a hammer and punch and told me I had to punch a hole at the bottom of the hot water bottle in the circle, so they could hang them up. She also told me not to talk to the two women beside me, they were sisters and they hated the Irish.

Well, I punched away all day; I loved it and filled one trolley. The man laughed and said I was working well and brought me another trolley. I got on well with the men and women there but kept away from the two sisters. Then one day, one sister was sick and fell down. I ran over to her and did something to her head and back and she was taken home. The other sister started talking to me and so did her sister when she was back at work.

She asked me what I had done to her that day she was sick. I laughed and said, "Oh this and that!" We laughed. I was '*told*' what to do, but how could I tell her that and the sister told me one day they had had a bad experience with some Irish years ago and of course they branded us all the same.

We got on so well. After that they baked a lot and used to bring me in some cake and buns to eat at lunchtime.

Paddy and I were getting on so well. I used to go to Church and one day I talked to the priest about the visions and things. He was very good and listened to me. He didn't tell me it was the devil or to pray more. He said, "No doubt God has a plan for you and when the time is right you will know."

This made me feel much better. As I was leaving him I felt a great lift off my shoulders – relief! Someone believed me. Then he said, "When you pray, will you pray for me." I looked at him, did I hear right? Was he asking me to pray for him? He said it again, holding my hand and saying goodbye.

"Yes," I said, "I will."

I was on the street laughing and ran and ran. Then it happened again, a huge picture in front of me. It was at the front door where we live - Paddy's brother on the right and another man standing beside him. I was opening the door when it faded. (Oh!) I thought, (it's happening again). A few months later the doorbell rang. I opened the door. It was Paddy's brother – Mike, and he said, "This is Billy from California, the eldest brother." I couldn't believe it. Just like I had seen and Mike was standing on the right. Bill was home from California on holiday to see the family in Ireland and had come to England to see us. He asked if we would go back to California to work. He would get us a place to live. After they left for Ireland we talked about it and decided to go. We set about getting passports and visas then we gave in our jobs notice to leave. I remember the two sisters started to cry when I said I was leaving. We were going to Ireland first to see our families then to California.

The morning came for us to leave. As we drove to Dublin for the plane I was sick. They had to stop the car twice on the way to the airport.

When we arrived there we left with no problems for New York.

As we got off a plane we saw people stopped at New York immigration. They were being sent back to Ireland. Paddy was afraid this was going to happen to him as he had been in trouble in Ireland for throwing a dustbin through a guard's window. But I was 'told' we would be alright.

We had to get another plane to Los Angeles. The snow was thick on the ground and the place was white. I remember saying to Paddy, "They told us to leave coats and heavy things, to bring only light clothes, what will we do?"

We got in the plane and set off again for Los Angeles. What a difference here! It was so hot - we laughed.

Paddy's Auntie and Uncle lived in Beverly Hills so we went to see them. There was so much food on the table, so many knives, forks and spoons. I said to Billy, "What do we use first?"

"Just watch me," he said "and follow, start from the outside and work in."

We were very nervous. There were lots of people there all talking about the parties they had been going to or what they had bought. One bragged of buying Bing Crosby's table lamp at a sale. As she talked I was *'told'* - *'some of these people are so false'*.

(Oh!) I thought, (not again, not here too!) With that I started to see 'inside' some of the people. One woman had a big red spot in her back, another had a black colour in her stomach. The colours around them were not nice. I wanted to get out as it frightened me. Then a woman asked me with two plates of bread in her hand, "Do you want sweet or sour bread?"

(Sweet or sour bread? - Oh my God!) I thought, (just give me a piece of bread). But I couldn't just take one. Then I *'heard'*, *'give us this day our daily bread'*. I have heard this in the church before in Ireland, but what does it mean?

I got up from the table and went out into the garden. It was lovely and felt so peaceful. As if someone put his or her arms around me. I asked God "What's going on?" I don't understand it all. Then I saw a tree swing and sat on it. A woman came outside and asked if I was going back inside to eat.

"No thanks." I said, "I'm not hungry."

After a few months we got a place to live in Alabama - Orange Grove country. We were told Paddy was working and the women next to us said, "There is a job going in a guitar factory, did you want to go and see?"

"Yes I do."

But Paddy's Auntie and friends said I was too nice for factory work and I was to get a job in the chemist. I didn't want a job in the chemist and I didn't know how to work the money yet. I wouldn't go to the chemist.

Then on Sunday Billy took us to a restaurant to have dinner. They would call us to a table when ready. As our surname was called out, everyone started to talk to us, asking us where in the old sod we lived and what's it like there.

At the table they asked us what we wanted to drink. I didn't know what to ask for. I didn't drink then. Billy said bring her a devil's something, I didn't hear the 'something'. I was thinking I am not going to drink this. When it came in a big glass it was yellow with a straw and froth on the top. They told me to drink it. (Oh my God,) I thought (I'm drinking this devil's stuff'). It was lovely and I wanted another but was afraid to ask.

As the months and nights went by Paddy was losing his temper with me. He wanted his rights in bed. But I was still so afraid. What am I going to do? I couldn't do it. I felt sick and started to get very bad headaches. I had had this in England as well.

One day we had gone to look around the big shops. We got into a Walt Disney glass elevator. We were told this is the only one around. Outside one big store there were lots of people on motorbikes, standing and talking. I was looking at the beautiful colours around some of them. One person I saw looked like one side of her was male and the other side female. I couldn't understand this. I hadn't seen it before.

Then my brother in law said, "Don't stare at them they are homosexuals and we can get a fine for staring."

I didn't know what it all meant but I knew it couldn't be too bad, as they had lovely colours around them. I saw pastel colours of blue, pink and yellow.

By now Paddy was getting very angry and I thought the best thing to do was to leave. I couldn't tell him what had happened when I was a child. He wanted us to talk to a priest here but I didn't like the aura around the priest and wouldn't go and see him. So I flew home on my own. They took me to the airport. I so wanted to stay. I loved him very much - I didn't want to leave him, but what else could I do?

I arrived home and just told my mam I wasn't feeling very well. Oh I missed him so much. Then walking down the street one day, I saw in front of me, Paddy at my mam's door. The light faded. I thought he is coming home. But he is getting on so well out there and I knew I couldn't go back to him, as much as I wanted to.

I got a job a few months later. Then while in the kitchen of the house, while drinking tea, there was a knock on the door. As

28

I got to the door I was being *'told'* - *it was Paddy*. I couldn't believe it. I opened the door and there he was with a big smile on his face. "Hello!" he said.

I burst out crying. We hugged and kissed on the doorstep. He asked me to try again and live with him and his parents and brother on the farm. I agreed as we couldn't live in my parent's house - there was no room.

I moved out to Avoca. I loved it - the animals and travelling around on the tractor. But it didn't last long. He wanted sex and we ended up fighting. He tried to grab me one morning in the bedroom. He frightened the life out of me. I jumped over the bed and out the window, down through the fields, running through the milking cows. I was shouting, "Help! Help!" to the workers. Paddy was running behind me. There was one boy working on the farm that lived just down the road. He thought he was hitting me so he came over with a shovel and hit Paddy over the head, knocking him right out.

"Oh Thanks!" I said, "I am going home." As I set off running down the road into town. I got into the house and told my mam he had hit me and I wasn't going back. What else could I say? I felt awful about it. I knew it was my entire fault and talked to my mam. I said I would be going to my brother and living in England. I thought he'd never find me all the way over there.

I did this and got a job in a fish factory, made new friends and grew to like the place very much. Then one day he was at the factory. He asked me to give it another try. I did, but it was of no use.

He asked me to see a priest, talk to someone. I agreed but I said, "Not the priests in Gorey. Alright he said we'll see our priest in Avoca. We drove down to Avoca, knocked on the door. There was not a nice colour around the house. It was very dark. But the priest was ok. I remembered him coming to the farm and asking Bill, my father-in-law, for a sack of potatoes and Bill would not give him any. At the time I thought that was an awful thing to do.

The door opened and in we went. Paddy did all the talking, telling him how scared I was 'to do it'. The priest asked me "did the nuns do this to you?" He seemed angry, saying, "Did they? Did they put this stuff in your head?"

I just looked at him. He said something under his breath. "They have done this before," he said. I thought (other people have been to see him about the same things). He went on talking to us for ages. Then he said, "This is God's house, the two of you can stay here tonight and try to work things out. You can have one of the rooms upstairs.

Then I was *'told' 'Don't stay in the house'*, quite loud. I looked at the priest to see if he had heard it, but no reaction. Then he said you go out and let me talk to The Traveller on her own. I caught Paddy's arm. "No!" I said, "I don't want to." I knew he was not the one I could talk to as his colour had become dark and it frightened me. I couldn't understand it all.

We got up to leave. Paddy couldn't understand why I wouldn't stay at the house. Coming out the door the priest asked again, "Look," he said, "go up the stairs and try to work things out."

I shook my head. Paddy shouted at me "Come on, let's try."

"No!" I said crying. That night in Avoca village we had a big row. He was so angry; he couldn't understand why I was like this. I walked away from him. I just couldn't tell him what had happened in my childhood - the abuse. I walked over to the bridge and stood looking at the river. He came over to me.

"Right! That's it!" he said, "I'll take you home to your mam. I knew it was finished now. I knew he wouldn't be coming after me anymore. But I still couldn't get over my fear.

There was no divorce in Ireland then. But the priest told me to get an annulment$_2$. I had to have a doctor examine me to make sure I was still a virgin. I remember the doctor, after the examination, saying to my mam in the house, "Did you know the marriage was never consummated?"

I didn't know what that word meant. Then I had to go and talk to the priests at the Bishop's house in Dublin. I won't go into this but what the priests asked me and said made me feel dreadful. Today I would call them 'Bastards!' At that time in the 60's I was afraid of them. I think most people were. I came away from the house feeling terrible. I remember stamping my foot and saying "I hate this fecking place!" and I never swear. I decided to leave Ireland once again.

Notes

The photograph at the beginning of the chapter is of The Traveller outside the ruins of an old chapel.

1.   *The place 'Gorey' is not the original location this having been changed for the purpose of protecting the identity of the writer, whom has been threatened on more than one occasion.*

2.   Annulment is voiding of a marriage that has not been consummated (when no procreation has taken place between the partners).

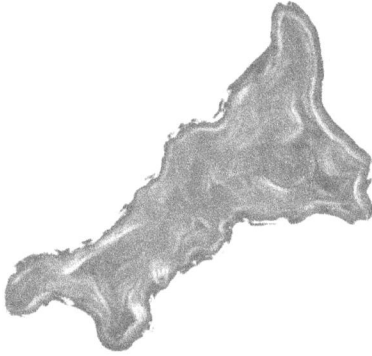

Chapter 3
Cornwall

I came back to Cornwall. It was like I was drawn there. I got a job and made friends. I worked at Sedgemoor Priory. The local people called it the old 'workhouse₁'. It was a place for the elderly people who were sick. I went for a nursing job but there was only a domestic job going. The matron told me one of the nursing girls would be leaving in a few months and to see how I get on and then change over. I was given a job on the male side.

I got on well with the old men. One man had cancer of the mouth and face. We would help him feed with special spoons. The side of his face was bandaged up. This man was lovely. I could see lovely colours around his head. He smoked a pipe, which he loved. No way was he giving this up. Then the time came when he could not light and pull on the pipe.

I was *'told'* to *do it for him*. I would do it when the staff weren't around.

Ray, the male nurse, caught me one day and said, "Paddy you shouldn't be doing this." He told me off in a nice way. He was the only one who ever called me 'Paddy' and it was ok coming from him. We got on well. I got on well with most of the staff, both nursing and domestic. I helped them a lot with the patients and I loved it.

I went on lighting the pipe, pushing the tobacco down with my finger and pulling on it to light it. All the men would laugh. Then one day I was coming down the ward to work and he was standing just in front of me. He had white light all around him now and it seemed to be glowing around the head.

I laughed, "Are you feeling better today, standing out here?" He was looking at me with a big smile on his face. He looked lovely. Then he said, "Thank you." The light faded and Roy and Les were in front of me.

"Traveller," they said, "Tom has just died."

"But …" I said, "he …" then I stopped. I was going to tell them I had just talked to him, but I couldn't tell them. I asked if I could see him. As they took me into the ward and behind the screens, there he was – dead - the pipe beside him on the locker. I felt so sad. I loved to help and talk to them all.

I remember one man had very dark colours around him. I started to talk to him one day, asking him about his family, where he had travelled, where he had worked and in minutes he started to get colour around him and the dark was fading. So I always made a point of talking to people when I could.

When anyone died people would open the window. I heard one woman say, "Let the spirit go free." But you don't have to open windows. I saw many times just before the person dies, the whole form of the person leaves the body from the head and is hovering just above them. Then if seen it just disappears through the wall. I saw Tom two days later. This time the colour was glowing like a warm, bright yellow light just around the head area. It felt so warm.

Again he said, "Thank you," with a lovely smile on his face and he had lovely thick curly hair. I never saw him again but I always said a prayer for him. I was always afraid to tell people of this in case they thought I was mad.

Then I started going out with a boy. I liked him, he made me laugh and I needed that. What stuck out most in my mind when I came to Cornwall to live - all the men carrying bags on their backs. I was told they were 'crib bags' to carry the food. They all worked for ECLP, the big clay firm. Their clay went all around the world. A boat brought it to Cornwall Pottery$_2$, where I used to work. I thought there were hills and mountains in Cornwall but was told they were only clay tips, some grown over with greenery.

I liked living here. The people were nice too. I spoke to everyone, as we do in Ireland but I was very shy. Then one day the matron and head boss - Mr Gibbs, asked me into the office. She asked me if I would go and do my training to be a nurse at St Laurence's Hospital – Bodmin.

I wasn't sure. She said I could stay there and come back every six weeks at weekends. Then not very many people had cars. She told me to go over and have a look. My boyfriend's father had a car and he took me over. It seemed miles away to me. Then going over the hill into Bodmin Hospital on the left I saw a huge great black cloud of smoke; not in the sky but in the buildings and right across the road to the other side. It frightened me. I started to get a headache. I didn't understand it all, but I knew it wasn't right. I said to my boyfriend, "No, I won't go in. I don't want to work here." We came back.

The next day I told the matron. "I don't think I will like it and I am going out with a boy and wouldn't like to leave."

She laughed, "Well, think about it and we will talk again." Then she asked me to change over to nursing as the girl was leaving. But I was fine as I was and liked the girls I was working with. So I stayed in the job I was in for a while.

After that the place was being closed down and the new hospital built so many left and the rest moved to Penrice. This place was so different. Everything so new, but I liked it.

I went on over the years *'seeing'* and *'hearing'*, helping people and still going to church. If I was working on Good Friday or Easter or any day I should be going to church I would ask for time off to go. They always gave me the time off. I would run to the church from the hospital, sometimes the Porters would give me a lift as they went on their jobs. But I Know many times they would just give me a lift down. They were very good. I worked with some lovely people, then one day when going into church I was *'told - the help is always there when you need it.'*

It was Good Friday. I picked up some papers to read and saw in big black letters **'I am always with you'**. I looked at the priest and looked back at the paper and it was gone.

This was to happen a lot over the years. Then I saw the big Celtic cross above alter and someone standing just by the side of the priest. It was getting brighter and brighter. I looked around to see if people were seeing this and was *'told' - they can't see it.*

As the figure got brighter I began to panic and get frightened. I was going to leave the church when I heard *"don't be frightened – look"*. As I looked up it began to fade. As we left the church when the service was over I thought the priest must have seen that! I'll go and talk to him.

One day I went to see him and told him what I saw and heard. I asked (his hand to his mouth looking at me) if he had seen it. He shook his head. I couldn't believe it. "You saw nothing?" I said again.

"No," he said.

Oh now I was sorry I had come to him. Yet again he told me of the devil and to pray, pray and pray.

"I do pray!" I said, "I pray all the time."

Then just like the priests in Ireland he said, "Throw holy water everywhere."

"I have done all that," I said, "and I wear a big cross."

He gave me medals to wear and to put under my pillow at night.

I said, "I don't dream this, I see and hear it in the day time, anywhere, even at work when I'm awake."

He told me opening the door, "I will pray for you."

As he said this I could see a black colour in and around him. I thought, (not again!) as I walked home. I felt dreadful. I wanted to cry but couldn't.

(What's wrong with me? Why is this happening to me? There is something wrong with me!) I thought.

When I got home I burnt some of the things I had written over the years. I was so mad and threw holy water all over the place and put medals over the doors. What am I going to do I thought? My head was in such a state.

The years went on. I was still 'seeing' and 'hearing' things.

At work I would be *'told'* to put my hand on a person's head, back, arm or leg then there would be a burning sensation in my hand.

I would see some people and know they were going to be sick or even die. Then there were some people sick and I'd be told there was nothing wrong with them. They would be picking up from second hand clothes.

I remember one woman I was talking to and I could see all these heads around her. I didn't know what it was. Then after a while she told me everything. She was wearing second-hand clothes, she felt more comfortable in them. But never the less she was sick, picking up bad vibrations from the clothes. I was told to tell her not to wear them and why. She was shocked but it got her thinking. Even furniture can cause negativity or if you give someone a present that wasn't meant for him or her, maybe bought for you and you didn't like it.

A card that people give and maybe don't like will have a dark aura around it. I always knew if a card or present was given to me with a good heart. It had different colours around it. My mam always knew this too.

Some people would be shinning all over, others just a tiny light by the belly button in the stomach.

I remember one day being *'told'* – *'to go pay the rates'*, a short walk away. I didn't want to as I was cooking. Again I was *'told'* to go. As I got to the road I was waiting to cross the busy road when I was *'told'* – *'look to my right'*, as I did two lads were coming

36

down on pushbikes. I was *'told'* to watch; as a big lorry came past one lad carried on. The other boy got on the inside of the lorry. The lorry turned into the road beside me, the boy and bike going under the double wheels. I screamed and the driver stopped.

A man stopped his car and came running over, he was a first aider. Then the other cars stopped. Someone shouted, "Go into the house and phone for an ambulance and police!"

The first aider pulled the lad from under the lorry. I could only stand and watch. His friend was now with him. Taking something from his pocket and putting it on his forehead. I wondered if they were brothers. Then I was *'told'* he was blessing him. I could see the colours around them, they looked good but lying on the road the boy's colours were fading.

I was *'told'* to go over and put my hand on his knee, but I couldn't do it. There were lots of people around now. Some had come out of their houses.

The ambulance came and was putting him on a stretcher and out of all the people the man looked around and asked me to help. I went over, put my hand on his knee and leg, which looked bent, and said, "You are going to be fine, nothing will be wrong with your leg. You'll think I am stupid but you are going to be fine – honest!"

His friend asked me for my name and address. The driver was in an awful state, he said he was coming up for retirement soon and this was the only thing that had happened in all his years of driving (catching my arm).

"If I hadn't heard you scream I would have gone over him again!"

The man had no colour around him at all, with the fright it had gone. Then we were taken into a house to have a sweet drink.

Weeks later I had a knock at my front door. Two lads were standing there and I recognised one but not the one on crutches. He told me, "I came to say thanks to you. I am fine; there was nothing wrong with my leg, as you said. They kept me in hospital for a few days and to use the crutches for a little while when walking. The driver is going to buy me a new bike, so all is fine."

I couldn't believe it; the lad I was looking at was called Tony. He was dark skinned; yet when I had seen him he was white! He told me they were Mormons from Salt Lake City, over here for a short time. They came to the house a few times after that.

After a time I changed over to the nursing staff, working on maternity. I was *'told'* - *some babies needed help* and I was to *'see'* some things. I also worked on the clinic side and one day I was calling a patient in to be weighed and urine tested. I had her notes in my hand. I shouted her name out. Two women got up laughing their heads off. I said, "That didn't sound right," with my Irish accent, laughing.

She looked at the cover of her notes. "Look!" she said, "that's my name there. I changed my name years ago. I haven't been called that name since school. The name I called her was covered over, so how could I see that. Then I was *'told'* - *The name you are born with, you die with, no matter how many times you change it.*₃

Then I was working in the room with the doctor one day and a women came in. I could smell₄ her. Something was wrong with her I thought. She sat down. Although she had colour all around her it was faded and not bright. Then the doctor told her she had cancer. I watched all the colour fall from her. She said she didn't want her family to know.

When she left I talked to the doctor (Mr G). I couldn't tell him what I had seen, instead I just said, "You shouldn't have told her that. It frightened her."

"She wanted to know that she only had a short time to live." He said.

Another lady came that also had cancer; it was cancer of the stomach. She had a short time to live also. I asked for help for her. I prayed she would be all right. I was told to put my hand on her back as she left. She kept coming back for check-ups. She lived eight years after that.

When she died I went to her funeral. I saw her in a beautiful golden light, standing behind the Vicar looking at people in the front row. Then she came forward beside the vicar on his right side.

One day in 1980 I was *'told'* quite clearly, *'Don't eat the meat.'* It was beef. I found this very strange, as I eat very little meat and the beef would be well done. I would always take the end slice, the burnt bit. I took no notice and still ate the meat.

Then out to dinner one Sunday there was lots of beef in the restaurant on a silver tray. We were all going to have it. It looked lovely and well done. Then I was *'told'* to watch, as people in front of me had beef put on their plates - *'look'* I was *'told'*. I saw red raw bits in the middle or on the edge of the beef. Yet to the naked eye it was cooked.

I asked the friends I was with, "Does the meat looked well-cooked to you?"

One said, "If they were to cook it anymore you wouldn't be able to eat it!" and they laughed.

I had the meat on my plate but I never eat it anymore. I was *'told'* it would be the same in time with white meat and in the end with fish - that *'this was all man's doing'*.

Then I was *'told'* - *join the flower group*. Oh, I thought. 'I can't do flowers!' I was *'told'* - *'I will show you what and how to do it.'* But I was still nervous and went to a demonstration on how to arrange flowers and bows and when it was my turn to do the flowers I was told what flowers to buy, the colours and how to do them. A lot of them were natural. Just from hedgerows and maybe a few bunches of flowers. But whatever I bought I paid for myself. I also put into the display little birds I had at home. I also put treated wood in, which I got from friends and family.

One day the priest came along when I was working on a display.

"It's lovely! How did you think of it?" He said.

I said, "It's all natural." Then there was Christmas and Easter. The money they spent on flowers I had never thought of it before but I was *'told'* - *'It's all wrong, all these displays. Just one is enough. People should come to pray and talk to God. Not to come to just see the flowers.'*

Sometimes the girls would play with the flowers for twenty minutes or more to get the display right. *'You should look at a flower for its beauty'*.

Another time I was asked to help a person with a flower display for another church. It was Remembrance Sunday. I was *'told'* what colour flowers to get and I also put three poppies on the display and a cross with a poppy on it.

Then I was *'told'* – *'this is all that is needed or light a candle in your home. There is no need for marches as most of the people that have died are reborn to learn again. They would be born in different countries and different families. Some that had killed each other would come back as brothers or sisters to love each other, as they had hated each other before. Yet not knowing this'.*

Again I was *'told'* – *'do not follow tradition. We must be free to make our own minds up. We came from God - we go back to God. What we do in-between is down to us and we alone will be judged on that'.*

I went on seeing TV type visions but never knew what they all meant, having been to all sorts of priests, missionaries and vicars

Notes

The picture at the beginning of the chapter is of Cornwall.

    1.   A workhouse is a place where people (including children) were forced to work and live if they became destitute.

    2.   Name of Pottery firm changed.

    3.   The name you come in with, you go out with and are judged with.

    4.   When The Traveller talks of smells in this case it is not a physical odour smell but a spiritual smell, and not sensed by the physical nose. Just like some people hear and see spiritual things with something similar to spiritual ears and eyes.

Chapter 4
Lourdes

Then on March 1991 I was *'told'* to go to Lourdes in September. I was told there would be a person to go with me and not to be afraid.

I never wanted to go to Lourdes in France. My mam and sisters have been there many times and asked me to go but I always refused.

Then one day, while shopping in the town I met a girl I used to know and work with at the hospital. She had left this job and I had not seen her for a good many years. We talked and then she said she would be going to Lourdes in a few weeks. I was *'told'* – *'this was the one!'*

"I would love to go!" I said, but I was told in September and she was going in May. I did not say anything to her about this. I

41

told her I would stick to her like glue when I was in Lourdes with her.

We had tea to talk about it all. I went to her home. We got on really well. Then she got sick and could not go in May and I was *'told'* she was well again. We went in September 91.

We were going to stay in a family run hotel, which she knew the layout of. I could not have had a better person picked for me to go with. As we set off on our journey, 13th September, we arrived at London, Euston train station.

We sat on the seats nearby. Straight away I was *'told'* to watch a group of young boys sitting in the circle of seats. With them was an older boy of about 26, very weather beaten, they were all talking, the boys were about ten to fifteen years old then I heard the older boy say "Don't look at him! Keep your head down. Don't even look up. Do you all hear me?"

"Yes," they replied. I watched as a man about 45 to 50 in a blue striped suite carrying a brief case walk all around them and then he walked down the platform. The older boy still telling the boys: "Keep your heads down!" Then the man in the suite came back again looking at every one of the boys faces. He did this a few times then walked away. The older boy said, "You are alright now, he has gone." Then I saw a shadow disappear. I was *'told'* the man was after the boys for sex - *'Bad time stuff'*.

As we were getting off the plane in France I *'heard'* - *"Welcome!"* I had just put my feet on the ground and I saw and felt a great mass of white smoke. It was huge! I felt a warm *'swish'* from it and this was lovely. I didn't know what it was. I looked around. There were only people coming off the plane. I looked at Sue to see if she saw anything. She was just looking around as I walked I thought of being here before - but I could not have ever been here! As we made our way to the hotel people were speaking French and I knew what they were saying. I could not understand this - I do not speak French. I was afraid to tell Sue. She would think I was mad. She knows I cannot speak French.

We arrived at the hotel. The feeling was lovely. Inside there was a group of French people talking and having a drink, as I passed them my thoughts were: (I know all of you). But, how could I know them, if never having been here. This frightened me a bit. Then I was *'told'* - *"Do not be frightened."*

It was early evening and Sue asked if we should go down to the grotto.

"Yes!" I said. I got a lovely feeling in my stomach 'tingling'.

As we made our way through the streets, I knew the way.

How could I know though? I could not tell Sue.

As we walked my head felt weird. It was about eight in the evening. There weren't too many people here now. But candles were being lit as I stood in front of the grotto. I was immediately *'told'* loud and clear *'You won't need to come here again'*.

I was so shocked. "I just got here!" I said.

Two more friends would like to come here and one friend with a dog. But I heard *'no more'*. I couldn't believe it. "I just got here!" I said again.

Next day we went to mass and to look around the church I went to light a candle. There was a crowd of women; they paid £50 to have a giant candle lit. Some people from their town in Ireland collected the money with good intentions.

Just as it was lit I was *'told'* - *'this is all wrong, if the person had lit a candle in her home or just a small one at Lourdes it would be better'*. I could not understand all this. We have lit candles all our lives and always in a church, giving money to have candles and a mass said. We attended the evening procession of prayers and hymns then I was *'told'* I don't have to do this again. This I also could not understand. This is what I had come for, I thought. Next day we went sightseeing to a castle.

My friend had made plans for all of the days we were there, but this day I was told I had to go alone. I could not understand this. We had plans to go to the pyramids. I could not tell her. Off we went on the bus, up to the mountains - it was beautiful! As we got out the bus driver spoke in French to us, I knew what he said - "Be back here at 5pm to leave and have a nice time."

I was afraid to tell my friend I knew what he had said. She would think I was fooling her that I could not speak French and I had been here before. One English lady asked me, "What did he say?" I told her when my friend wasn't there with us. We looked around. It was then 5pm.

Back on the bus, as we went down the mountain I became very sick. I had a plastic bag someone had given me and I kept getting sick in it.

Then I was *'told'* – *'get off the bus'*. But I don't know where I am, I thought again I was *'told'* *'get off the bus'*, the driver stopped and I got off. I told a friend "You stay on the bus, I will be fine. I can't stay on the bus like this." (I felt awful). My friend was mad, "you can't walk!" she said "we are miles away." As soon as the bus drove off I was fine. The terrible sick feeling had gone. I was *'told'* - *'Now walk!'* As I walked the place was changing I have been here before I know this way I went through places I had never been or seen before.

Yet I knew this place. I was *"told"* I know it like the back of my hand. I arrived at the hotel. Sue came running out. She was mad. "How did you get here?" she said.

"I walked," I said. She did not believe me.

Next day I was *'told'* to go down to the baths and what time to go. She told me we couldn't go now. The place would be packed. But I went and she came with me. We did not speak. She kept looking at me funny.

We got to the baths. There were only a few people there. She could not believe it. As we waited to go into the baths I kept sinking. I could not move off the chair. The sweat was pouring off me. At that moment in front of me visions appeared of people fighting, dressed differently and pulling two wheelbarrows with wooden drums on them. Some men were pulling two wheel carts. People were being burnt, women and children running and screaming. I was being pulled away, and then it faded. I was shaking and crying my eyes out. I couldn't move, my friend did not know what to do or say then she said, "Sometimes this place has a strange effect on people!"

Then we were called to go into the baths - I could hardly move from fright. Two women had my arms. I went into the water, but I was *'told'* to get out. I told the women

I could not do it and that I would come back later. But I did not go back. Next day I went to the grotto, just to walk around and think (what's going on?)

On the last day I was told to go to the first church (a little one). But my friend had made plans to go on a trip and we were being picked up by bus. Again I was *'told'* to go to the church. I just could not say to her "no". I had done my own thing opposite to what I said I was coming here for.

We waited and waited but no bus came. Yet again I went and did what I had too. As I got into the little church I sat for a minute - what was I to *see*? Then I was *'told'* look at the nun in front. It was so sad, the nun had to sit here every day in the front seat, near the alter and the Blessed Sacrament. I was *'told'* – *'this was a terrible waste of a "Human Being", she is not growing at all'.* On the way back I met a lovely Irish man. We got talking, he told me he had been coming here for years and would like to have company. I asked: "Have you ever asked anyone or asked for help to find someone?"

"No," he said.

"Well," I said, "start asking!"

I meet a woman from England, she said she wanted to start a shop and hire a place, but the Catholic Church would not let her.

Well I went to talk to some priests in Lourdes about what had happened to me. Some never knew, others told me to pray. But one said, "God will let you know of His plan, if he has one."

When I came back from France I could not understand all that had happened there. Again I asked the priests – (no they didn't understand it either).

Then one day I was *"told"* to go to the library. I went. As I entered I asked, "What am I looking for?" I was *'told'* to walk to my right over to the end as I did I was shown a round red aura and the words came up "The French Revolution". I said, "I do not know anything about this." I was *'told'* to take it and read it. As I got into the book about France the scenes I had *seen* in France were in this book about the Catholic Church burning the people "The Cathers[1]".

I could not read any more, it upset me too much. At one point the bishops said, "Kill, burn them all God will know his own!" All the people running, screaming and being burnt, the same vision I was shown in France. I had gone back in time but I did not know that then. I could not believe that the Church would do such things in God's name.

After the visit to France the visions became more and more. One day I was *'told'* to look out of my window as I did I saw lots of houses, trees and a viaduct. Suddenly there was nothing there. The sky and all around had become very red. Then I saw huge crosses falling from the sky and I was *'told'* – *'I am burning the churches down - as you sew, so shall you reap'*.

This frightened me, (what's it all about?)

Notes

The photograph at the beginning of the chapter is of candles at Lourdes.

1. 'Cathers' or Catharism was a religious movement with Gnostic elements that originated around the middle of the 10th century France, branded by the contemporary Roman Catholic Church as heretical.

Chapter 5
Raising Money for India

Subsequently, one day there were three of us in the car when suddenly in front of the window a beautiful white bird appeared. We were driving along yet the bird was gliding with us. As I went to say to the others: 'look at that beautiful bird, I wonder where it came from?' I was stopped. I could not talk. I was *'told'* - *'they can't see'* - so they could not see it.

I went forward to look all around. The bird with its wings wide-open, eyes like sapphires so blue and the feathers so white - there was not a mark on them. The feathers were so small and neat. Next it was like a cloud, like writing it said *'The Holy Spirit'*. Then it all faded. I looked outside and all around but I could not see anything. One of the people asked what I was doing.

"Oh Just looking around," I said, "it's a lovely day."

Again I went back to the priests. I went to see them about the beautiful vision of the bird and the writing - 'The Holy Spirit'. In the Church they say 'Holy Ghost' instead of 'Holy Spirit'.

I am getting fed up knocking on their door about all this and all they would say was "mmmm…" no one else could see it.

I said, "That is what *I heard* out of the three of us in the car."

The priest was sitting listening to all this, and then I left.

In 1993 I had a huge vision. It was completely blue in colour.

I saw myself on the roadside, full of potholes and very hot weather, looking at myself on a bus, yet still in my home.

I told the priest again of this vision but he only put oil on my forehead.

I was *'told'* – *'you have to go to India to see and hear what is going on'.*

I was in such a state when the vision faded. I said, "No way! No! I am not going! I don't even know where India is. I am not going!" I stormed out of the house. I was crying. "I can't go to India. How can I go? I know nothing about it," I was saying as I walked and walked, still saying, "I am not going. How can I go to India?"

As the months went on I was seeing coloured boys, girls and women and I again saw the bus. I saw a train and myself sitting by a window with a hole in it and it all cracked like a bullet hole. I saw myself walking in a heavy rain, mud all around my feet. I saw myself sitting in the sun. I saw the people standing in a certain way, the colour of their clothes, the way the women had their hair. Then I saw a nun in white, bending down and calling me to a flower. I thought this is what I saw as a child, a black face with a white habit. I thought at the time they were dead people. I wondered what's going on, all this is really scaring me.

I was fed up talking to the priests so I went to see vicars from other churches to see if they knew anything about this. As I talked to one vicar in his home there was a red aura around and inside of him.

He looked at me, after I had talked to him for a while. He said he felt anger.

"Do you see any colours around me?" He asked. I was afraid to say 'yes'.

Then he said, "No, no there are no colours around me. Do they talk about Jesus Christ in your church?"

"Yes," I said, "of course they do." He walked across the floor. He stood for a minute in the middle of the room. Just then I saw a huge hand above his head, the hand turned up to face me. I saw a little black dot in the middle of his hand and I was *'told'*, 'he has not grown one bit, he is stuck'. I was *'told'* to leave. As I got up he carried on talking and asked me to come back again. As I was leaving his wife and child came. I could see the child was not well and was *'told'* what it was but I was afraid to say. I just said take him to the doctor tomorrow. I did go back again he said he saw a big difference in me from the first time and that they had been praying for me. I was *'told'* - there was no difference in me.

The wife did tell me she saw the doctor about the boy. She had lovely colours around her as she told me this. I did not go back there again.

I have been to so many different churches. I saw many priests, missionaries, vicars and lay people over the years about visions and messages. I would rather they say "we don't understand it all." Most churches years ago put down other churches and told me to join theirs but I was always *'told'* - *'NO!'*

I went to a unity church service. One vicar got up and talked and I was *'told'* – *'he would not know if I was standing in front of him. He is so full of his own self-importance'.* Another Vicar stood up, my gosh I could see right through him. He was shining and the colours I could not describe. I was *'told'* talk to this man in the future.

Again I was *'told'* – *'you are to go to India. The people need help and bring the people together as one'.* I said, "How can I do that? How can I do that? I do not know anything." Then I was told symbolically your path will be cleared. As the whole scene faded I felt so low. I thought to myself how on earth can I go to India and what does all this mean?

Time went on. I left my job and started another. I was *'told'* to leave the job as I would get no help here. I thought help for what?

Then one day a friend came down to the house, he told me "I have done a terrible thing. I thought I'd better tell you."

He had been to the West of Ireland to see his family. On the way back on the boat he got talking to a man. This man said he was a priest and working with Mother Teresa helping the poor in India. As they parted he asked for my friend's address so they could keep in touch (I do not suppose he's even a priest). My friend said he was sorry and he does not know why he did it but he gave him my address instead of his own. Again he said he was sorry then he said, but we will not hear from him so don't worry. A few weeks later the letters started to arrive. I passed them over to our friend then I was *'told'* to ask the priest if I could help. So I started getting letters then I was *'told'* – *'he is just a link in the chain'*. I did not understand this either as we wrote to each other this priest seemed ok. So I wrote to him about some of the visions. I was *'told'* just what to write to him about.

Then a letter came asking me over to meet Mother Teresa. This was March 1994.

The priest said she also was a messenger for God and I could talk to her. I could not believe it then I was *'told'* again, you are going to India and you will talk with Mother Teresa and again was *'told'* the priest was just a link. I did not know what it all meant but I was so excited I couldn't believe it at all. I sent money over but now I was *'told'* I would be going there for the 1st September 1994. That was in a few months!

Then I was *'told'* "ask" the priest what they need. What is most important to them and I would try and get it. He wrote back and said a jeep. He told me the price of a cheap jeep, and the expensive one, the better one was double the price. I was *'told'* to go for it.

I thought the Catholic Church will help me. Then I was *'told'* I was to go to the church and ask just to put a poster on the notice board. To say what I was doing, raising money to buy a jeep for Mother Teresa, not to show the letter from India, to do it on

50

trust and the Priest's help. As I got to the Church I was very excited, it was Easter. The flower girls, to whom I was a member, were doing all the flowers for Easter Sunday. As I was talking to one, I was *'told'* look at all those flowers, this is not right.

I remember thinking we always do this. I talked to the woman telling her I was going to India to see Mother Teresa and what I was going to do. I said, "I am now going to see the Priest. Is he in?"

"Yes," she said.

Off I went around the side of the church. Putting my left hand up to press the bell (I felt different) then I was *'told' – 'you will get no help here'*. I could not believe it and it was so loud and clear.

"Yes, I will," I said out loud. "It's the priest's house, it's the priest house," I said it again.

The door opened and I asked the priest, "Could I talk to you for a minute?" I explained it all and asked, "could you please put a poster up on the board for me." I remember thinking well this is a bit different from talking to them about visions and messages.

The priest still looking at me said, "What do you want to do this for?"

"What?" I said.

He went on to say, "What about our church building funds there are no poor in India. What do you want to do this for?"

I could not believe it. I had raised lots of money for the Church over the years and a friend made all sorts of woodwork, which I sold at work to raise money for the Church. My family and I cleaned it years for free. I bought bricks for the Church. I thought I certainly did my bit and more and now I was asking for a bit of help myself and it was not here. The priest did not like me asking to put a poster up. I was to ask for no money it had to be down to the people.

Then I was *'told'* to tell him of the visions. I said, "Father God wants me to go to India. I do not know what for, but I have to go. I was *'told'* again to tell him of the dove - the beautiful white bird and the visions telling me to go to India.

Still looking at me and then he got up and walked. After a few minutes he said, "All right but you do not use Mother Teresa's name."

I said, "but in the visions it said it is for Mother Teresa. I was to see Mother Teresa again."

He said, "No you will not use her name." Then I was *'told'* ask him to write a poster.

I said, "Father, you write for me, tell me what to put."

"No," he said. "You do it."

I was *'told'* again to get him to do it. I said, "Father, I am not good at putting things together. Please will you do it?"

I could not understand why I had to get him to do it. He got a pen and wrote on the envelope one part. I did not agree with it and he changed it. "There," he said, "get that done and comeback to see me."

As I got up to leave I felt dreadful. No different from the way I felt as a child asking them what the visions and messages meant. Both here and in Ireland as I got outside the door there was a beautiful light and a staff just standing within the light.

I looked back to see if the priest could see it. I was *'told'* he could not see it. He shut the door.

Then I was *'told'* you are going to do this in the weeks ahead. I am going to make you stronger and stronger. You are also going to see more. As I walked to the car the awful feeling I had with the priest had lifted. I was feeling light and happy.

When I went back to see him they were expecting a visit from the Bishop and everything in the church had to be right. I asked to see the priest. He was not there so I talked to the other priest. I asked if he knew about this trip to India and he said, "Yes, they had talked about it." I gave him the poster and asked if he could put it up or if he wanted me to do it. He said he would read it and do it. I told him I did it as Father D₁ had asked. As I was talking to him, I was *'told'* the Bishop's visit is more important to him.

I had got on quite well with the two priests in the past. We had a laugh and joke together at times. Now it was as if I did not know them.

Within the next few days I was shown a vision and *'told'* now I will show you who will help you. I was shown a moving white aura around a figure. I felt the grace and beauty from this person yet I did not know who it was. I was 'told' I would see it at the church. I went to mass over the weeks ahead looking at the notice board every time but my poster was not on it and I could see no one at the mass with the aura. I even went to other masses at different times but nothing. Then there was a Unity Service, people talked from other churches.

I went and was *'told'* to sit on the left hand side, a few seats from the back, as people came into the church. One man who had been very ill sat beside me. I felt this moving sensation from me to him it was 'blue'. I was *'told'* he needed help. This man always sat near the front of the church. With that this man came in. I could not believe it. He had the lovely white moving aura around him. He walked to some people and sat three or four rows from the front. As he got up to speak it was lovely. He was still glowing.

I asked the women I knew beside me who he was.

"Is he new here?"

She told me he was a Quaker but his father is Catholic.

She described the father to me but I did not know him. Then a huge light came up with him and his father standing beside each of them. I could not believe it. I looked at the woman - she did not see it. Again I was *'told'* she could not see it. I had been to all the masses and no one had the aura I had seen in the vision, only this man – 'a Quaker'; out of all the Catholic Church and all the people - I could not believe it.

Then I was told you are going to have your eyes opened as never before in the coming months. I left the Church that evening knowing the poster would not be going up.

I felt so disappointed with the whole thing. Now what was I going to do to raise the money? I had needed seven thousand pounds!

On the way home I cried. The voice I had been listening to all my life was right. I got no help from the Catholic Church. The priests did not want to know but if I was doing it for the Church funds, well that was different.

One day I was told to ring my mam in Ireland and tell her what I was doing and about the priests.

"Oh that's them all right," she said, disgusted with them. "I'll help you," she said and she certainly did. She walked the streets of Gorey, telling people what I was doing and if they would help. She had coffee mornings and sales. People were very good to her, after all I was not living in Ireland and I had left as a young girl.

My mam is a healer and people came from all over to see her as far away as America and Africa. As people saw her, they would leave money for me for India.

People in my church, that I had known for years, said they could only help me in as much as they were able because of the priests. I could not believe what I was hearing. I was *'told'* to listen and say nothing but I felt so angry. I was *'told'* to see my old friends. They all went to the pubs and clubs - which I did not.

One Sunday morning out walking I was *'told'* - *look over there!* As I did there was five pounds on the ground. I was *'told'* the first start for Mother Teresa. Then I was *'told'* to open an account and *'told'* who to go to but I would be told when.

Thank God, he gave me good friends who did care. The jeep appeal went on the radio and papers. There were coffee mornings, auctions, bring and buy, male voice choirs, sponsored walks, cake auctions, beautiful cakes making a lot of money for the appeal.

I wrote to the priest in India and told him the priests would not help here so it will take a bit of time to raise the money. I got letters back and he was asking for my phone number. 'No', I was *'told'* quite clear, not to give him my phone Number. I did not know why, but I went along with it.

As the weeks went by I was *'told'* to ask some people for help. Then there were other people asking me if they could help. The ones I thought would help did not, the ones I thought would not help did - it really surprised me.

The money started to come in, then at a musical/proms evening the woman I was told to see was at this event. I was talking to a man and he said, "I will introduce you to Paddy."

We got talking and it came up about an account needed for the appeal. She told me to come and see her. She was head of the Bristol and West, which I did not know.

I did go and see her and set up the account. It was opened on the 2nd of April of 1994 with one hundred and sixty five pounds. I put the five pounds I had found into this account also.

People helped me over the months. Most of the people were great, but I was *'told'* to change some. I was shown, as I saw the people, I was *'told'* – *'this is how you see them now but I will show you how I see them'*. Some looked terrible, black auras and I was *'told'* – *'they're worth to me is a little as a five pence piece'*. And I *'saw'* the five pence piece in front of them.

"Never judge a person on what they do or the clothes they wear, I will show you more in the future."

In four months only, I had raised three thousand, seven hundred pounds. Over two thousand pounds my mam, family, friends, neighbours and people of Gorey had raised.

When I got a statement from the building society, I was *'told'* to send it over to the priest. I did this. Again the Priest wrote back when he received this and said I was doing very well and asked for my phone number, again and again I was *'told'* not to give it to him.

I was *'told'* to leave my job I had being working at for years and go to another place to work, as I would get more help there and I would be of help to them.

I never knew what it all meant. I soon found out. The elderly people did some beautiful paintings and other craftwork. I was to get them involved in the place and people. Most of the staff were wonderful. They had a cream tea day; the cooks worked hard cooking all the scones then the auctions at the Hotel Porth Avallen and Exhibition of paintings and prints of local artists.

The elderly residents were taken to see their work on display. They were so excited. I was *'told'* – *'look at those faces, see how they have changed'*, and they had - their auras, were shining. They were doing something different. I was *'told'* – *'we all need to be doing something - no matter what our age'.*

I spoke to a couple of the girls at work about the visions I was having of India.

Then the time came to have all the injections. I had them no bother. It was like the needles never touched me.

I was told wherever I needed help the help would be there. The people would be there. Then I got the name and phone number of the Quaker I had been shown in Church. I phoned and said what I was doing and could the man help. His wife said he's very busy with a lot of his own work and would not be able to take on anymore. I asked if I could talk with him, well there is not much point; he won't be able to help. I said thanks and put the phone down.

Again, when fund-raising, I was told not to show the Indian letters asking me to meet Mother Teresa. The people had to take it on trust and this was very hard. I wanted so much to show the letters. Some people did not believe it. People would say you might see her. I would say I will be seeing and talking with her. So everything was done on trust.

I went around to the Churches but got no help. I was *'told'* – *'they are all doing their own thing'.* As I was going to another Church at St. Stephens, I was *'told'* to turn back. I would get the same response from them all. I was *'told'* to go to Truro Cathedral to speak to someone there. I went down and asked to talk to someone about what I was doing and if they could help this time. I was *'told'* to take the little painting of Jesus with me. Canon R came out to see me on the 9th of May 1994. He smiled and said he would see what he could do. I heard no more.

On the same day I was *'told'* to see the Catholic priest at Truro Catholic Church. He said all he could do was put a piece in the newsletter, well I thought that is more than my own church did.

I was *'told'* I would hear no more.

Then I was *'told'* to write to the Bishop C in Plymouth. I was not to tell him what happened at my church just to say what I was doing.

He sent me a letter back and a cash donation wishing me a good trip. Then I was told now write back and tell him what happened at your Church, I did. I heard nothing back

One day I was *'told'* to go to Roche Rock it is on the edge of Goss Moor. I had heard of the rock but never been there.

As my friend and I got there and looked around we were just leaving when I heard a bell ring. As I looked back, I saw monks in brown habits, heads bowed and arms in their habits crossed. They were in line and walking out and around to their right. I could still hear the bell and then the scene faded.

To my surprise weeks later a painter gave me a framed sketch of the rock. He said it is a one off and to auction it to raise money. He asked, "Do you know where it is?"

"I certainly do," I said, "it is Roche Rock."

We auctioned it one evening but the man that bought it left that evening without the picture or paying for it. I was *'told'* to pay what it had raised and keep it. I did this.

As the Bristol & West statements came in, I was *'told'* to send them to him, the priest but no way was I to give my phone number.

Then on Thursday 25th of August 1994, my friend phoned me (the Bristol & West Manager) Paddy had been trying to get hold of me all morning.

I had been working. I had to go and see them as soon as possible. So my friend and I left for the building society. She told me they had a call from India to say make Bristol & West cheque in the name of the 'Roman Catholic Church'. A priest phoned and said the name of the place to send it to. I told them, "No way!" I knew the Catholic Church was not to have it.

I told her, "No!" again but I could not get it in Mother Teresa's name. The priest here in Cornwall told me quite clear don't use Mother Teresa's name. So I had to put it in the priest's name. However, I would make sure when I got to India it was for them both. I was told Mother Teresa gives a lot of things away. I was going to make sure she did not give this away.

Notes

The picture at the front of the chapter is of The Traveller and Mother Teresa.

1.   Name changed for privacy.

Chapter 6
1994 Calcutta – India

In 1994 I was given four names to ask for help. I have asked one so far.

After a very long and tiring journey from Cornwall I had arrived. As we were touching down, we were told over the

Tanoy[2] not to take any photos around the airport - it was very small.

There were queues for visitors and I made my way to the queue. I showed my passport and tickets to the lady. I had a photo of Mother Teresa in front of the passport, as she saw this she said: "Mother Teresa!"

"Yes," I said, "I am here to meet and talk with her."

"Oh! How lucky you are to meet Mother Teresa. She is a very special person, very wise."

"Yes," I said. She handed my passport back with a big smile. I went to pick my bags out. I had also brought a Casio (large one) with me, for the priest, he had asked me in a letter to bring one.

I had been *'told'* I was going to Calcutta, India, to *'see'* what was going on. I had no idea what this meant. I was not prepared for what I had to *'see'* and hear in the coming weeks.

As I got my bags and Casio I put them on a trolley. As I went to walk the Casio fell off the trolley. As I went to put it back in the trolley two uniform men came over to me. They were very pleasant but asked me about the Casio. I told them I was going to meet Mother Teresa but the Casio was for a priest. I had his photo and showed it to them.

"So it is new?" They said.

"Yes."

"Have you got documents?"

"Yes."

"How much did it cost?"

I told them, "£129.00."

"You will have to pay money to us too."

"But I haven't got any Indian money," I said.

I was getting panicky now, as I was explaining to them that I could not change and get Indian money in Cornwall, England. We had to get it in India.

He told me again that I had to pay money. It was very hot and I was beginning to sweat with that. I saw and felt the beautiful light and feeling my head went forward to see two bear legs from the knees down golden brown sun shining legs The hair and legs were shining then I saw he was wearing sandals, my head still down. I saw the two men stand to attention and salute they talked, I still could not see the man only the legs; with that the two men came over to me packed all my stuff arranged it better and Casio on the trolley and wheeled it out.

I could not believe it! As they walked away from me, they smiled at me. I was so nervous; as I took the trolley the Casio fell off again. I packed it on quick afraid of my life they would come after me but as I looked back they were still smiling at me I smiled as I went out of the airport. There were lots of people at each side (no one inside) they were waiting for people. As I came out I thought 'God I hope the priest will be here again'. I was *'told'* not to worry. With that I saw the priest. I was so mad, his aura was not very nice, it was dreadful (all black and quite wide). I shouted and shouted to myself, 'why didn't I see this?' Why did I not see this on his photo and I was *'told'* if you had have seen it you would not have come and that was true. I would not have come.

I was so angry. His aura took me back many years to my home in Ireland.

Then I was *'told'* to watch his eyes. The first thing the priest looked at was my trolley; with one question on his mind – 'did I have the Casio?' He was standing behind a string of rope holding a lot of people back from the doorway.

As I got to him, "Oh good!" he said, "you have the Casio. Come, come." As he came around to me and took my arm he said, "Welcome to India."

There were about twelve young boys with him. They followed us to the waiting cars at the airport. I thought the boys were from his church. The smiles on the children faces were lovely. They were glowing and all had lovely colours around then. The rain came down - it was so heavy. I got soaked but within minutes I was soon dry from the heat of the hot sun. I did not know what to expect as I knew nothing of this country.

A car stopped in front of us. The driver put my bags into the car. The priest shouted to the boys in Indian. The boys backed away. The priest was angry with them. I could not think what for? They were doing no harm. We drove off. I thought, looking at this priest I had just met, (I do not like you. You look and feel horrible).

I had felt so happy to be coming here with all of the money raised for the Jeep and the Casio. My friend and I had bought the Casio and now looking at him I did not know what to expect. I saw a lot of this black colour around some of the priests in Ireland, nuns and bishops when I was growing up and it never felt good. When I saw different colours it always felt different and better.

The priest asked, "Have you got the cheque?"

"Yes," I said. He smiled. Oh he felt terrible and his smile/face looked awful. I thought (Oh my God! I am here for weeks what am I going to do?)

Then he said, "Whom is the cheque made out to?"

I said, "You."

The smile broke across his face again, still horrible. I did not even want to talk to him as we drove along looking out of the window. I saw lots of people living on the pavements and the poverty was dreadful!

I said to the priest, "This is awful! - The poor people."

He laughed, "It will shock you."

We arrived at a big gate and drove in. I saw nuns in white. 'Oh!' I thought. This is the Mother Teresa's Convent.

I said, "Is Mother Teresa here?"

"Oh no," he said, "not here. I will take you to see her in the morning."

We went into the kitchen. A nun came in.

"Oh Father! Tea," cups of tea were in front of us and a nun brought a fruitcake. Oh it was lovely. Two more nuns came in, said, "Hello," and walked out again.

We were alone.

From outside I heard the birds singing and a lot of children's voices. The windows were wide open. The priest asked, "Have you got the cheque here?"

"Yes," I said, "I have two, one from Ireland."

"I will have it now."

"Now?" I said, "Not tomorrow with Mother Teresa?"

He laughed, still smiling. I gave him the cheque.

He looked and said, "You have brought a lot of money into my country and in such a short time."

"Yes," I said, "people in Ireland and Cornwall were very good."

Then, he stood up, "Right we go now!"

I finished my tea quick and out the door we went, down to the main gate.

"Where are we going?" I asked.

"To get you a bed," he said, "down the road."

I thought to myself you have done all this before. I was *'told'* - *he has*. Close by was a little crowd of people by the gate. There were also a few nuns there. As the priest spoke to them telling them he was taking me somewhere to stay. I saw one nun light up all white around her.

"Oh Father, I will ask if she can stay here." She came back with Mother Superior and said, "She can stay here."

(Oh thank God) I thought. I felt safe here. I had seen nuns in white in my visions, but it was not these nuns but the nun with the light all around her. We became good friends. She was a good one.

I said, "Thank you!" and they took me to a room. The Priest said he would come the next morning and collect me at six o'clock in the morning to see Mother Teresa.

I thought six o'clock in the morning was very early but I said nothing. That night I could not sleep. I was afraid I would not be awake and ready by six o'clock. I need not have worried as I was in a convent and the bell started ringing at four o'clock in the morning. At five-fifty in the morning the priest was there. I was ready. I got into a taxi.

On the way to see Mother Teresa I could not believe it. I was told in the vision I would see and talk to her on the 1st of September and here I was on my way to meet her. The priest said there would be mass first and I would meet her afterwards.

We got to the convent and walked up the lane to the brown painted door on the right. After a knock on the door a nun opened it, bowed to the priest, and said, "Hello!"

The first thing I noticed was a picture of Jesus on the wall, similar to the picture of Jesus I had brought here with me.

The priest told me to go up the steps and I would see him later. There were a pile of shoes outside and I noticed a sign saying, 'Only Catholics to take Holy Communion'.

I took my shoes off and went into the chapel. It was very basic - a big statue of Our Lady. There were lots of nuns there and some aid workers and visitors. I knelt down. Then out came the priest with another priest and said Mass. Mother Teresa was to my left, as I looked around. It was lovely to see her after mass.

I was taken to a room with the priest for breakfast - fruit and eggs. I was '*told*' just to take bananas. They were very small. I had not seen any like this before but they looked good.

All things have an aura around them. I usually know what to eat and what not to eat. The bananas tasted good. The priest ate everything. He kept telling me to eat more but I was not feeling hungry.

"Do I see Mother Teresa now?" I asked.

"Yes, soon," he said.

Then Mother Teresa came in. She looked so small but her aura shinned - not all nuns auras shined.

As the priest talked to her, she was looking at me.

"What is your name?" she asked. I told her. I said about talking to her on the phone.

"I know," she said, "yes, yes." She was not feeling too well. "I have a fever;" she said and was not talking too much.

I gave her the painting of Jesus that I was '*told*' – '*it would be the only thing she would want*' and also a Rosary of Cannamara Marble, my mam had given for her.

She thanked me. With that the priest went to talk to the other priest. I was '*told*' - *now ask to see her on your own.* I asked her, "Please can I comeback and talk to you? God brought me here to see you."

"Yes, yes, you comeback," she said. "I am here." She caught hold of my hand and put her other hand on top. "Comeback tomorrow," she said. Then she said, "take" looking at my camera - we took a few photos.

"Thanks," I said as we left, "see you tomorrow!"

She smiled. It was like I knew this woman. I felt something between us. I wondered if she also felt it? Could she 'see' like I can? The way she looked at me when we first met - she 'saw' something. As we walked out there were lots of people coming in to see her. As we made our way down the stairs and outside it was packed with men, women with babies in their arms and children all begging for food or money.

The priest pushed them away but they really looked hungry. I felt so sorry for them.

Next morning the priest came to pick me up early. He was leaving this day and wanted the Casio to take with him but I was being 'told' not to give it to him. But what could I do now? I could not tell him not to take it. I got it all ready for him and he would pick it up later.

We went to Mother Teresa's Convent again. It's a big place, we had mass and I talked with her. She told me to come back later that day. Benediction was in the evening and I love that better than mass. As I would be back later I went to the children's home before the priest was going to collect the Casio and go for the train. I was to meet him within two week's time. I loved being with the children and picked them up and let them look out of the windows.

Then I felt a tug at my leg and another little girl wanted a lift. As I went to put one down and the other little girl up - she would not let me go! So I had two up with me, one in each arm.

They loved it. Then they all wanted a lift. We fed them, changed them, and played with them. There were no toys anywhere just a big old couch upstairs to play on and some birds in a cage by the stairs.

The children just wanted someone to play with them and pick them up. Some of the nuns were very gentle; some were very hard.

Then it was time to leave. I made my way back to where I was staying. I had tea and was getting ready to go to Mother Teresa's convent for benediction. I started to walk and I was 'told' not to go.

"But I have to go," I said, "Mother Teresa knows I am coming and I want to go. I have been looking forward to it and everyone knows. Now if I don't go what would the nun say?" So off I went again. I was *'told'* not to go, but I did not listen and kept going.

Then I was *'told'* quite loud and clear to turn around and go back. I was furious but I did go back. As I was approaching the gate I was hoping no one would see me. (What would they say? Going through the gates - no one here? – good), I thought. Normally there are always people at the gate and a man to stop anyone coming in. I sat in a little room on my left and waited. I was asking why I was brought back.

No answer. Minutes later I heard lots of voices. Oh! She is not here. She had gone to Mother Teresa's Convent. I heard my name so I went out. The nun was shocked to see me. "I came back," I said.

There were men talking to the nuns, "what's wrong?" I asked.

This man was the taxi driver sent here by a priest. A friend of FR X₁, the police had stopped FR X getting on the train with the Casio. They wanted to see the papers to say it was his. They wanted the receipt for the Casio (I had put it in the Casio box).

The taxi driver had a letter from Mother Teresa's Parish Priest to the Mother Superior to read:

"Dear Sister Mary, The Traveller from Ireland bought the Casio for Fr. T₁ to use in his mission. He was stopped by police at Howrah Station, for not having the proper papers for the Casio. Then the police stopped the taxi and fined them 500 rupees for carrying an instrument without proper documents. Kindly tell them to refund 500 rupees to taxi driver and keep the Casio with her."

But Fr X did not say what he had told me in a letter - to bring the sales receipt with me, so the police would not let him take it on the train. He told the taxi driver to take it back to Fr RP₁ and to get me to see Mother Teresa about it.

But they did not do that, they went off with the Casio hoping to sell it and get lots of money but police stopped the taxi. They were fined for having the Casio so they had to go to the Parish Priest with it and then to see me.

The fine was 500 and 30 rupees. I paid, as the men did not have that money. The 30 rupees was for the taxi fare. I asked for the letter and the nun gave it to me I was *'told'* to keep it.

The next day the priest called to see me and told me Fr X had phoned him to tell me to take the Casio with me when I go to see him and that I had to see Mother Teresa to get a letter from her office to say I could take the Casio with me.

I said, "I will see her later in the day". I was *'told'* – *'4:00 p.m.'* as I made my way to see her.

I was appalled at the poverty in India. I thought the further I went it would get better but it got worse and worse. As I arrived at Convent Lane there was a young woman with a baby in her arms asking for food. I was *'told'* to stand back and listen. The nun on the door turned the woman away. I could not believe it.

Then some boys were asking for help for their mam who was dying of cancer. They were also turned away. I was told to talk to the boys. They were two brothers asking for milk. They had no father. They told me their mam was very sick. They asked, if I wanted to see her, she lived nearby, but I was *'told'* not to, just to get milk for them. They took me to a little shop nearby. I paid for the tins of milk and they went off.

"I'll see you again," I said. They were smiling. I went inside the convent and looked at the nun. She gave me a big smile but her aura was not too good. I asked to see Mother Teresa as I went up the stairs to her. I told her of the Casio and said the Parish Priest told me to see you. I explained the earlier situation.

Mother Teresa took my hand, "I am not going to write anything," she said. " *'They'*, told me to get the office to do all that but God is telling me to do this for you." She took me to the office typewriters clicking away. She asked the nun for paper, she gave her paper and pen. Mother Teresa took me to sit down, you write, she said, her address was on the top of the sheet of paper.

We talked about what to write for a few minutes then I wrote:

Dear Mother, I bought one Casio from England for Fr. T. to be used in his mission. I need you to sign to say he can have it please.' She told me to sign it and put the date on it.

Then she took the pen and paper and wrote: *'You may let Fr. T. use the Casio'* and she signed and dated it too. Then she told me to put it away.

I felt she was worried about something. I asked her if I could talk to her about the visions. As I told her something she told me, "I do nothing now *'they'* won't let me."

"Who?" I said.

She looked at me with big sad eyes – *"they,"* she said again.

Looking around, I asked, "Is the priests - 'they'?

She said again, "I don't see anything it's all taken away."

"Oh my God!" I said out loud. Is this what I had to hear?

With that a priest came in. She told me to stay. He asked her to sign papers she never read them and he never told her what they were, as he moved the papers I was *'told'* to watch.

"Sign here, here, here."

Some looked like cheques. When she finished he just got up and walked off.

"It's like that all the time," she said.

Then some priest came in, "We want photos taken with you Mother," they said.

She got up to walk away. "No, no," she said.

One priest said, "Mother!" in a firm voice, "we want some photos taken with you."

Oh I could have cried for her. I wanted to tell the priests to "Fuck off!" but I was *'told'* only to watch.

Mother Teresa walked back to them, held herself straight, two arms down by her sides, no smile and they took their photos and left.

I could not believe it. "Why did you do it?" I asked.

I was mad, "Are you afraid of them?"

She did not have to answer I could see she was. This was a world famous woman and yet whoever was running this place, she had no say and she had to do what she was told.

I asked her, "Do you do anything?"

No, she said, "It's all done for me, all taken away."

She got up and went to the office again, asked for something, she brought me a prayer card with her photo on it and said *'they'* did this too.

"You did not want this done?"

"No," she said, "I only want to help and feed the poor."

"Oh!"

The most beautiful light appeared on her head. I was *'told'* to bend forward and kiss her head. As I did she came forward. I could feel the purity of the woman. She smelt so clean and fresh.

"Will you come back?" she said.

"Yes, I will. I will always come back."

She let go of my hand and I walked away.

Outside as I was walking, my head was spinning with what I had witnessed in the convent. I thought (Mother Teresa is being used!).

I asked, "Is she being used?"

"Yes," I was *'told'* loud and clear.

I was *'told'* there was a lot more I had to see.

As I worked in the children's home, one day I was *'told'* - *'get your bags and leave.'*

I was shocked, "I can't," I said, "the nuns and children will see me and miss me." Again I was *'told'* to leave. I saw a white mist come over the room.

I was *'told'* to go. I could not believe what I saw and all the children just sat down, the nun writing at her desk. I was *'told'* 'she will not see you.'

I walked through the children not one of them reached for me.

I got my bag and left. As I got outside there were queues of people waiting for food. People were coming to the convent doors all the time, day and night, for food.

Then I met one of the priests I had met earlier.

"What are you doing today?" he asked.

"Nothing," I replied.

"Right you come with me and I will get someone to take you around." He took me to his church where I met another priest. It was also a boy's hostile. He gave me tea but the boys were out so he said, "I will send them to you tomorrow and you can go to town."

As I as leaving a young girl was coming and she looked so poor but she had a lovely face with a big smile. He took his umbrella and lifted her dress, laughing.

He said, "Look at her, she needs new clothes."

I thought how horrible he was to say this in front of the child. I put my arm around the girl and said, "Never mind, it is not what's in the clothes, it's what inside that counts!"

The priest did not like what I said.

Next morning, just after six I was waiting for the boy. The girl on the gate called to me. Frank had come for me, "Are you ready?" he asked.

I felt as if I'd known this boy all my life.

"I am ready."

"We have to get a bus, the Calcutta traffic is dreadful and so many people."

I asked, "Are you on your own?"

"No," he said, "Sambhu is also with me. He is across the street waiting for us." As we walked away he said, "There he is!" As I looked across the road I could see it was the boy I had seen in my vision, standing with his hand on his hip looking to the right and in the same clothes - I could not believe it.

As we crossed to him I introduced myself to the two boys I had seen in the visions at different times. Now they were here with me, so I knew I was ok.

As we travelled they talked of all the places around us. We reached the place we were going to. It was way out of town. I met more people - they were very poor and had nothing. They could not send their children to school.

I asked, "Don't the priests teach you for free?"

"No, no," they said laughing, "the priests don't help."

I met a man dying of TB. He told me in the cold weather the priest would not let him stay in the church out of the cold.

They all had to stay outside, even in the monsoons.

He asked if I could get him into Mother Teresa's Home. I said I would ask. He had been there once before. I gave him money for food and clothes, as I was *'told'*.

I found out on my second trip. This man did not get into the home. He died and was buried in the paddy fields where he worked along with thousands of other orphans. This is how all orphans are buried like this I was *'told'* and other people know they go this way as well.

As I made my way across the yard to the shack-out house, to where I saw the beautiful light, I had a little shock; the priest put his hand on my arm to stop me.

"We don't do that," he said. But a force was pulling me, far greater than him or me, it felt warm and lovely, like a huge coat of armour. I was not afraid as I was pulled away from the priest and walked on my own but I knew I was not alone. It felt as if I had an army all around and beside me, protecting me.

As I got to the little shack I heard the voice say 'look all around'. I was shocked at the state of the shack but more shocked to see what it was used for. This was where all the priest meals were prepared and the two lovely boys, so thin, with lovely big smiles prepared the food. Not only that, they slept here on the floor to cater for him. To be there for the click of the fingers, to be physically and mentally abused and then of course sexually abused too. I was *'told'* show no emotions just thank the boys. As I put my hand out to shake their hands and say thank you for the food, it was lovely.

The priest even tried to stop me doing that. I have not been in India very long but I could see as I travelled through Catholic grounds all around India, the same story everywhere.

I was taken to another church, which was huge like a cathedral. It had statues so big with gold crosses. When they have electricity on them there is flashing floodlights. The pulpit had gold crosses on it. One cross was a 124 feet high. There was one nun in this church (reminded me of the nun in the church in Lourdes just sitting watching) I thought they are all the same.

Churches put up leaflets to get people to come in. They tell a story of someone being cured and all the people pile in. People bring in loads of money with them. Shops are built and hotels are built. The poor people make most of the holy stuff in the Catholic Church sweatshops and it becomes a vicious circle.

I was taken to yet another church for tea. I was *'told'* - *just watch*. As we sat down for tea at a huge great table, a boy of about 20 years old brought in a tray of tea. As we finished I was *'told'* to put my cup back on the tray with the other empty cups, as I was going to do this, the bishop stopped me.

"It is not your job to do that!" he said.

I could see he was getting angry. I said, "Oh! I was only helping."

"No, no, no," he responded, "the boy will do that." With that the priest and nun apologized for me saying I do not know their ways.

While they were talking between themselves, the boys came in. I was *'told'* – *'look!'* As they picked up the cups not even looking up at us they were walking around like zombies. I could see they were afraid of these nuns and priests. I was the only white person there. Why did they not look at me? If it was the other way around I would have looked at them. The Bishop spoke in Indian to them but they were afraid to look. He was an arrogant bastard! His aura was black and he never spoke to me after the cup fiasco. He looked at me as if I was a bit of shit.

The bishop said something to the boy; he picked up the tray and was walking away when the bishop shouted something to him again. The boy bowed his head to him said something like 'yes' and left.

Then I was *'told'* - *their spirits are broken from years of abuse*. Now I know what it means to *'keep quiet and watch'* when I am here. Later I found out if they talk to us they get into trouble. The boys and girls are not allowed to say anything to visitors.

Then some people (I knew I could trust them) I had seen in visions took me to what we call sweatshops. There were young children making carpets in a cramped long shed. It had a few little windows at one side but the heat in here was dreadful. The children were so thin, their little legs bent underneath them. Over the months in India I was taken to many of these places. Children making all sorts of things in appalling conditions and they all said the same thing - that they belong to the Catholic Church; that the priests give them very little to eat, sometimes nothing at all for a day. In one sweatshop the children thought they had not eaten for ten days. They very rarely got paid and there was no water to drink. They worked from 4:00 a.m. to 7:00 or 8:00 p.m. but at Christmas and other times, they have to work until midnight to get orders out.

Then I was taken to terrible areas. I was so shocked - the people had no food, no water and no electricity. The ground was so worn over the years there was no grass or greenery. Some of the people had some rice drying on the ground. They told me that was all they had. I was taken into their huts. There was just a string wood bed, no blankets or clothes and a little stone made fire. Some had candles, others had no beds at all and it is so dark inside and of course the worn ground that a lot of the families had to sleep on. If they have a bed off the floor all the family sleep on it getting away from all the creepy crawlies and rats. The people are just surviving. Most of them try to work, picking fruit, spices and all things that come to western world. They get paid pennies for it.

I was *'told'* – *'it's time we opened our eyes. To look and listen, see and hear what's going on and act upon it'.* The Indian people are so afraid and yet very holy. They won't speak out - If they do speak out they will be beaten, kicked out or disappear.

So it is up to us to speak up for them, until the time comes when they can talk for themselves.

Then I was taken to Catholic owned shops selling all sorts of things that had been made here in India and going abroad. Some were brand names! (The brand names were all going abroad but being made here).

People told me that many items are from China with 'Home Sweet Home' written on them – they are not being made from the country they are being sold from. *'People want to buy it.'* I was *'told'*.

Then I was taken to a children's orphanage but it was not for the children anymore, it was for drug, alcohol and sexual abuse. Priests that were found out were not excluded from the Catholic Church but instead sent to this place for a time. It is a place where they do nothing, have everything done for them by the young children, whom are also abused. Then they are sent to work in poor countries where no one knows them and they have all they want and still have poor people kissing their feet.

One place I went to the children had bent down to kiss the white priest's feet. I was *'told'* – *'the people should not have to do this'*. I told the priest, you should just shake hands but he ignored me the smile that went across his face when the little girl kissed his feet said it all, he loved it!

Then I was taken to see the used clothes that had been sent in. Some priests were handing them out to young girls. They were taken to a room to try the clothes on in front of the priests. I was so disgusted but I could not say anything, as I would get the people who took me to see it all in trouble. I was *'told'* again *'the priests like young girls'*. They are often abused after trying on clothes. They came to me crying in the night.

One day I was taken to 'The Home for the Dying'.

I found this place dreadful. No one had a name, just a number. I asked one lovely woman I was feeding fish to, "What is your name?" she just smiled. I asked her three or four times and she would not answer me. She just pointed at her nose.

She took my hand and put it on her head, "Will you come back here?"

I could not answer her. I just smiled and kissed her hand. I watched another woman having a bandage taken off her leg. She was screaming in pain, as the bandage came off so did a lot of flesh, leaving a big hole in her leg. I shouted out loud, "Oh my God!"

I felt a hand on my back and a pot with four tablets placed in it. I was told, "Give it to 39!"

Next I had to wash a woman who had been very hot all night. As I washed her gently the nun pushed me to the side and threw

74

a bucket of cold water over her, scrubbing her hard with an actual scrubbing brush. The woman screamed out, shouting at the nun, but the nun did not give a damn, even with me staring at her.

I said to the aid workers there, "This is a bloody disgrace. I would rather stay on the street! As I came to find out a lot of the people are "taken" off the street and a lot do not want to go into the home. After what I saw and heard. I would rather stay on the street I know someone would give me a drink or something to eat - I saw it happen.

Mother Teresa nuns told me they see their families once every ten years but she has hundreds of nuns from all over and they are all moved around. All the airfares come out of the donations. All the nuns have to be kept at the convent, and two nuns do airport duty and caring (when she was sick) for Mother Teresa, priests and visitors from the airport to the Mother Teresa Convent.

Mother Teresa told me she did not want to choose any nun, she said it was God's job, but she was told to pick a successor.

She also told me to come out and tell the world what is going on, she put her hands up in the air, "Tell the world, tell the world what God wants them to *know!*" She took my hand, "Come we will pray together, ask God what to do."

We both sat down, side by side. It felt lovely as we prayed together for God's guidance.

I told her, "It's not time yet to tell the world, to do what God wants."

She said, "but tell the world!"

"I will," I said, "I will."

She said it again, "Tell the world and Ireland." I thought that was lovely '… and Ireland' – we both laughed.

I was *'told',* - *'we are to look back only to learn from and go forward to heal.'*

Some Indians called Mother Teresa *"Agent of Pope"* but I found she was afraid herself of the hierarchy. The bishops and priests are the bosses of the Church.

In England the news of dead babies organs had come to light and they all had parents. Orphans have no voice at all. Orphans told me: "We thought when Mother Teresa came, she would talk up for us, but we still love her."

In some areas people have to queue up for hours for a bottle of oil and then it has to last them for one month, cooking for a family of four to six people.

Little babies were dead and thrown in dustbins, some with marks on them.

Notes

The photograph at the beginning of the chapter is of the same painting of Jesus given by The Traveller to Mother Teresa. (Painted by Greer Hawke 1994)

> 1. 'Fr' means Father, it is also another name for a priest and the 'X' is a change of name for privacy.
> 2. 'Tanoy' means the airports loud speaker for public announcements.
> 3. A 'Monsignor' is another name for priest.

[The below is an unedited extract (except the name being replaced) of a written letter by one of the monsignors, of the Pope to the author about all the injustices of the Catholic Church].

Letter from the Vatican, 23 November 1995:

Dear 'Traveller'

The Holy Father duly received your letter and I regret that, owing to the immense quantity of mail addressed to His Holiness, it was not possible to send you an earlier reply.

His Holiness appreciates the concerns which prompted you to write to him. He will remember you in his prayers and he invokes upon you the sustaining grace of our Lord Jesus Christ.

Yours sincerely,

Royal Mail® Great Britain
Recommandé
signedfor
international

RI 5358 2441 2GB   Sig req

RI 5358 2441 2GB   Sig req
RI-5358-2441-2GB
PRIORITY HANDLING & REGISTERED DELIVERY

Royal Mail
POSTAGE   PAID   UK
09/05/05   £3.72   PL25
433539   1-1903289-1

His Holiness Pope Benedict XVI
The Vatican,
Rome,
Italy

The above is evidence of the original letter sent to the Vatican and the reply given above (see page 218 for the original letter sent to the Pope).

ST. JOHN'S CHURCH

CALCUTTA

Ref. No............... Date 02 : 09 :19 94 .

Dear Sister N

The Traveller , from Ireland
bought Cassio & was given to
Fr T   to carry to Allahbad.
At 'Howrah Station, Fr T
did not carry it & left it in
the Taxi as he had no papers.
The Taxi driver was caught by
police & fined Rs 500/= for carrying an
instrument with out proper
documents.

     Kindly tell The Traveller to
refund Rs 500/= to the Taxi
Driver & to keep his Cassio
with him.

     Sorry for the troubles.
with thanks   Fr P

02·09·94 -

Letter from taxi driver handed to The Traveller.

MISSIONARIES OF CHARITY
CALCUTTA ██████ INDIA

03-09-94

Dear Mothe

         I Bought one cassio in ENgland & gave it to FR T   to be used in the Mission in Allahbad I need you to Sme to say he can have it. Please, FoR Church

The Traveller

You may let Fr P use the cassiou.

lu Teresa m c
3-9-94

The letter above is from the original for Fr T, with only the names being edited for privacy.

Chapter 7

The Journey North

Then I was '*told*' I was to visit another priest. I did not want to go it was two days train journey away and the priest was awful. He also had a bad aura. Then one evening I was in my room and I saw a huge light as I sat on the bed. *From the light three robed monks with white light, about one inch, going all around their brown robes came walking towards me.* (I could not see their faces as their heads were bowed and their hoods covered their head and foreheads). *Their hands and arms were clasped together under their habits. The first two were big, the one behind small, a lot smaller.*

They stood in front of me and told me not to be afraid. To pack my bag, I was going on a journey. I felt so at peace then. The light faded, I could not believe it. I felt so at ease and I was not afraid anymore. I got up and packed my bag.

I was *'told'* to go on the Friday morning. I got up at 4:30am and went to mass. The first hymn was 'Do not be afraid'. My friends came to take me to the station. They stayed to make sure I got on the right train and they also checked that my name was on the list of people attached to the outside of the train. Then it was time to get on. My friends got on to find my seat. As we got to the seat number I could not believe it. Just as I has seen in my vision in England, I was sitting beside the window; it had a hole that looked like it had come from a bullet and was cracked in places. The only thing different, there was a man sitting beside the window. But I still thought it was still good to see this. Then my friend, holding my ticket said to the man, "This seat is taken."

I said, "Oh! It is ok. I will sit in this seat."

With that the man jumped up and said, "No, no this is your seat, please sit."

So the vision was right. I told friends in England about this vision. I just wish I could have taken a photo of it but I had no camera. I had been told to leave the camera in the bag. I had also been told to leave my bags at night in case anyone took it but I knew I would be ok.

On the train I met a lovely couple. At night the husband told me to take the middle bed/seat facing his wife while he slept up above and below the other men slept. They looked after me on the whole journey. The train journey passed quickly at each stop. Young and old people would get on the train selling all sorts of things and playing instruments. I arrived at my destination - the station was packed with people.

I was the only white person there. I could not see the priest anywhere everyone was looking at me. I did not know what way to go so I followed everyone who got off the train. It was so hot and like Calcutta I saw so many lovely auras. The colours were out of this world as I walked on I was *'told'* to stop and wait. I was looking around for a short while when a man came towards me and again it was the same man I had seen in my vision - he had coloured clothes and a hat (all what I saw).

I said, "Hello."

He said, "The priest sent me for you, to pick you up."

I walked off with him feeling quite safe. As we arrived at the priest's house there were huge grounds, beautiful tropical flowers and lovely birds singing. They had beautiful colours. It was like they were welcoming me. They flew before me, around my head, landed on the ground in front of me and then they flew around me again. It was like they had gold strands of string coming from them, going around and around me. This was north India. It was so hot here. There were so many lovely butterflies.

Oh! I loved India. If felt like home, even here in a different part of India. I could not understand these feelings as I only have these in Ireland and yet I felt so content here. Then it changed as I saw the priest coming towards me, a big smile on his face but I was looking at the aura - not good.

I was brought back to earth with a bump. Exactly when he shook my hand, it felt bad.

(Oh!) I thought, (I don't want to stay with this priest.) He showed me around, I felt scared. Why should I feel this? I thought. I was *'told'* to come here.

Then he said, "I will take you outside."

I first noticed a big TV satellite dish on the roof and I was surprised to see a TV, as I understood he had nothing.

As we went across the garden, to a building, he said it was the Church, but not for long as they were going to build a new Church.

But this church looked fine to me. Then we walked to another building - it was a school. All the classes for this school were for the army, police and all the upper and middle class children.

I asked, "Do the poor children, come here?"

He smiled, "No, no," he said, "I will take you there tomorrow, to the villages." Then he said, "The school is shut because of all the unrest."

"What is wrong?" I asked.

"Oh there have been a lot of killings of the clergy and some traders want to put their stalls up outside the front of this building and we won't have it. It is going to court; we can't let them (people) get the upper hand."

Then I spotted a nun with her back to us. She was beside the flowers. As we walked towards her, the priest shouted to her. When she turned around I could not believe it, this was the nun I has seen in the vision and then she said what I had heard in the vision, *'Come and look at these lovely flowers'*. Even the colour of the flower was the same as I had seen in the vision.

As the priest introduced us he said, "I have told the sisters of your coming."

Again she said, "Traveller come, look at this beautiful flower." I could not help it I could not speak. I looked and touched the flower.

She said what it was called but I could not hear her. It was like I was floating away. I could see myself with the nun before me but in another time. She was a white person then and we were really good friends. As she took my arm, I was back again.

"You are very pretty," she said. "How was your journey?"

"Fine," I said.

"Come, come in and have a drink it is so hot for you." She took us into the convent. I met other nuns they were so young and looked and felt so innocent. Then the nun said, "She can stay here Father, with us."

Oh! I felt so relieved. I looked at her and said, "Thanks very much."

"I will show you your room."

The priest came too. The room was lovely and clean but there was a red mist in it and I felt fear but not for me.

The Catholic school was closed in the area because of the unrest and murders. Convents got dogs in to try and keep trouble out. A man would go on a walkabout with a fierce Alsatian dog. You could feel the fear in the area.

I was told not to walk around on my own. I walked around the grounds and one day walked to the big front gates. As I did policemen were beating young boys with their batons.

It was awful the boys were screaming I asked the priest to stop them. He smiled and said, "No, the police said the boys had burnt an effigy of a government official. They had to be tough, a lesson so that no one else would do the same."

I had a good night sleep and woke up four o'clock next morning. I watched the people coming in to work in the convent then I walked around the grounds looking at the banana and coconut trees.

There were all sorts of fruits and herbs. I watched a young girl scraping a coconut - it tasted lovely. The young girl was sitting on a piece of iron and scraping the coconut with the other end of the iron - it was a painstaking task.

I talked or said hello to the people as I walked around. Then some people saw me at the gate and shouted to me. I went to talk to them then the priest came and told me not to talk to anyone or go out on my own without him.

"Can't I go out and see things?" I asked.

"No!" he said.

Then a nun called me for breakfast. Bananas picked from the trees and coconut just picked and scraped. Oh! I could live on this and coconut juice.

As the nun told me her name, I shook her hand. I felt a ring I looked at her hand and this also I saw in a vision - just a hand and this ring. I had never seen a ring like this before, so I knew she was also ok. Not all the nuns were angels from my stay.

I saw very poor villages with no water, electricity and very little food. I saw the mud huts built by the people and a mud built school. There was nothing in the school, just a mud floor and darkness. This was a far cry from the schools in the church grounds.

In the mud huts people just had one set of clothes. Only a few huts had one single bed all the family slept on, off the floor from insects but most of the people slept on the mud floor.

I asked the priest what he was doing for the people.

"Building a new church for all to give them hope," he said.

"But the people need food, water, sanitation, clothes and beds - they need help!"

Then he took out a bag of small sweets and told me to hand them out – two each to men, women and children.

Oh! I was so mad I felt so ashamed to do this. I told the priest after giving out some sweets; I could not do this anymore and that the people needed food.

He took no notice of what I was saying. I was *'told'* to shout out again about *they need food!* He told me to keep quiet and said, "We don't do that," as we left the village.

I told one lady I would be back tomorrow and to watch out for me. When we got back to the priest's house I asked the driver to take me to the village again. He said he would call for me the next day.

As the driver picked me up I took some trusted friends that I had been shown in visions with me. We bought lots of fruit, rice and bread. Another rickshaw came with us carrying the food. Oh their face when they saw the food and no way was I going to take photos of this.

I was also *'told'* to give the women in green some money. I did this and we left - the Priest knowing nothing of all this. I said, I would be back to help them.

Then I was taken in another direction to other villages. They had so little space to live. I was *'told'* the priests had taken their land, for churches, convents schools and growing fruits, vegetables and herbs - they got nothing in return.

The villagers were told by the priests to give the land up for theirs and their ancestors' sins.

Again I was *'told'* to keep quiet about this or the people would be beaten or killed. I could not believe what I was hearing now. I could see why the priests had such bad auras.

Then I talked to more villagers in yet a different place. I was told they are called 'Rice Christians' by priests and other religious elders.

The Priests offer them rice and water if they change to the Catholic religion. Some of the Indians do this then the priests stop the food and water when the people have become Catholics, causing a lot of unrest among them. Their own people don't want them and the priests don't either. Then they are used for slave labour within the church for little food for the rest of their lives.

I was taken to Churches that were being cleaned and painted inside and outside. I watched young boys and men with sandpaper scrubbing the church buildings. The dust was terrible as they scraped the old paint off. They looked so sad. One boy was called over to me. The man told him to show me his fingers; he had rubber finger gloves on. He held up his hand. His fingers were all swollen. He tried to take off one rubber finger cover; it was stuck to his flesh. As he pulled it I nearly died. The boy cried out, his fingers were all cut and bleeding and he had to work like this.

I asked, "Do you get paid?"

"Very little, sometimes nothing," I was told.

Then I was *'told'* – *'churches are being built on the sweat of the people'.*

I watched another place where women were digging the foundations of a new Church being built and carrying the heavy soil and stones on their heads. I was told the priests wouldn't pay for a lorry to take the soil away, so the people carry it away.

I also watched people with no shoes on their feet digging and making red bricks and the priest telling them, "Do it for God."

Then I was taken to sweatshops, shops, hospitals and research centres owned by the Church.

A priest told me that the sisters of charity run some of the sweatshops - only they did not call them that.

Then one day, I was taken by a priest to look around. There had been lots of rain in the night. As we drove through villages the rainwater was three to four feet high.

There were no drains and I was told it gets a lot worse than this. The smell of the rain and sewage was terrible. The priest told me to get my camera out and I started clicking away.

"Click, click," he said, laughing, "it will get us a lot of money in."

Then the priest told me again, not to tell the sisters what I had sent to him. The priest said, "We will stay well away, don't tell them too much."

I went to places where they were making clothes for ladies and gents on old singer sewing machines.

We went down lanes. I could hardly breathe with the bad smells and these poor people had to work in this from dawn to dusk.

There was also children working, making: balls, toys, garden things, ornaments, bags, purses, wooden beds, quilts and pillows₁. They did not stop. It was so hot and with the rain, there were so many insects. I was walking on them; they were crawling all over the people's bare feet. There were lots of white maggots and flies all over the little children. There were huge rubbish dumps with the men, women, children and animals searching for food. I thought my head was going to burst.

Then we called at another place the people had white rabbits about twenty in a pen. I said, "Oh! You have some pets."

They told me they have them to eat. "Oh!" Some rabbits had their legs broken with their eyes all running with matter.

Before I left for India, I was *"told"* to take my cross and chain off. (I had never taken it off) I was also *"told"* not to take my medals and rosaries. I was surprised, as I had always had them on me where ever I went. I was *"told"* - *"trust me!"* I did. I took everything off, left it behind what made me trust was, when I put my finger on the priest doorbell when I went for help and I was *"told"* – *'you will get no help here'*. It took me back to my childhood when I rang the doorbell in Ireland at the priest house and I was *"told"* the very same thing. Now I know where and who makes all this stuff. I threw everything in the bin when I got home.

I talked to young girls that had been burnt by the nuns. One girl had the burn mark on her thigh for wetting the bed and being sick all the time and she could not tell them she was being abused!

I watched as young girls went for confession. Some were in the room for ages. I did not wait. One was so long when I spoke to her days later, she told me of the things the priest was doing to her. I told her next time she goes to tell him, he is not to do this, God said it is wrong.

I found out if girls speak up or try and stop the priest or Christian brothers the priest tells the nuns. The boys and girls are in trouble and they move them or if the girls get pregnant by the priests, the nuns are told the girls are after all the boys, which is not true. I found some priests and nuns children are being looked after by other orphanages and are getting sponsor money in to help them and they are looked after.

One priest called me out from the nuns and asked me, showing me a photo of a little boy; could I get a sponsor for him? I said I would try, he said, the women worked for him. I later found out the women had other children too.

I found people came to adopt babies and men came to the convents to get a girl to marry. They wanted fair skin girls; the very dark girls get left behind. Some get taken into employment into the church and are abused but cannot do anything. If they make a fuss they get put somewhere else or kicked out on the streets. I also found the sisters of charity arrange marriages which I was *"told"* – '*they have no right to do this'*.

While I was out walking one day, going down one street, but *'told'* to go another way, a man was coming towards me. His aura was white, wide and blazing with movement. I was *'told'* to follow him. As we walked through the lanes and alley ways the poverty was getting worse.

I was *'told'* - *no one comes down here*. The smells were dreadful. I saw little children with sores all over them. Then I came to fields of tobacco. I asked, "What are the other fields?" they were different.

I was *'told'* they were marihuana drugs. I was *'told'* again there were young children working the fields. There was a crowd of people around me.

I was shocked. I asked, "Who owns these fields?" No one answered.

I asked again louder. I could see the people were very afraid, "Who owns them?" I said again.

One voice said, "Look around you what stands out most prominent in the area."

'Oh God!' I thought. I did not have to look at the church and bank as I said this people walked away. I was walking behind the man I followed in here, he was going back a different way

Then there was sugar cane, fields of it. I could not believe it, and yet the people are so poor. Again I was told the priests take the land off the people or they tell them to give it up for their sins.

When I got back to the priest house, the strange thing was he told me he had to go out for a while. He had land to register.

I found the priest was doing this in a few places I had been to. When he came back he did not see me in the other room reading and I was *'told'* to listen. He phoned someone and heard him say "Your lordship, I have just deposited another ten thousand dollars."

The person with me told me that was for the poor but the poor will never see it. I came across this often here. In the visions God *'told'* me I was going to have my eyes and ears open as never before. I now know what that means.

The next day the priest said he had to see a man about some land and again he was smiling. Then another person I saw in a vision came into the yard and said, "Come."

As I followed him I was taken to a village and shown a small hut. I was *'told'* two men were inside and the priest had told them there was a spell put on them by a witch and if they left the hut, they would die.

I could not believe it. I said, "That is rubbish! I will go in and talk to the men." But they would not let me go into the hut.

The people have to work on their land they don't own anymore. On all three visits to India land was taken from the poor people. My last visit was in South India.

The Church had accumulated so much land in 1998. I told the clergy how they got it and why people are killing themselves. You will not see any of this in your Catholic books or papers

Then I was taken to another hut. I was told the young man was a lovely boy, worked hard for the priest and was good to the village and his parents.

One day he came home mad and would not work or leave the hut. I asked again, "Can I go and talk to him? This time they said, "Yes."

The boy, about seventeen years old, was on the string bed with a blanket over his head. He was so frightened as I put my hand on his leg, he jumped up frightened, shaking, as I talked to the man beside me. He talked to him too.

After a long time, we came to find out the priest had abused him. The hut was full of people. I was *'told'* look at his mum. Looking around I was thinking, I do not know his mam as my eyes went around, I saw her tears flowing down her face.

Then I was told of the people beating some of the priests, burning them alive and cutting off private parts and tongues. I was told this was happening all over India. This is the fear I had felt and all the red coloured anger.

The priests got the young girls pregnant and then the babies were taken into the convents. But I also talked to nuns that had left the Church. The bishops and priests too had sexually abused them also. A lot of the young nuns can't leave the convents. They have to put up with it. Then I was taken to a convent where I saw the pregnant nuns and other nuns who look after the babies in other orphanages.

Some young girls asked, "What happened to your leg?"

"Mosquito bites," I said.

They explained that they had never seen bites like that. I did not want to say it was a rat. I had to go to a doctor. My leg was in a terrible state. I had more lumps coming out of it. They would burst and blood would come out. The doctor gave me tablets. He wanted to send me to the hospital but I said I'd be going home soon and I would be going to see my own doctor[2].

I was glad I had tea tree oil to bath my leg in. I also washed it in salt water.

Some children told me their Mammies were the nuns. I watched as the nuns came to see them on Sundays. My head was in torment at the peoples' suffering. The priest's and the Church are a law unto themselves.

The joy I felt coming here was fading fast. This is my Church, the Church I was brought up with and did everything for, not questioning it at all. Now I am coming to find out that I am ashamed of it, ashamed of being Catholic, ashamed of being white and ashamed of what they are doing to them. I called the priests pigs but that is not fair to a pig. They never hurt anyone - I can't find words to describe these priests and nuns who abuse their authority. I think, 'first-class bastards' would fit.

One day there was confession. The nuns were telling everyone where to go. I was shocked as I saw a beautiful blue light and I was *'told'* to go to confession but only to 'tell' of what I found out about the priests. It was in a big room, a priest was sitting behind a brown screen. As I walked to the chair to kneel I saw the priest's aura around his head, it was black and brown - it looked so dirty! I had a shiver, and then I started my confession. I felt great warmth around me as I told him some of the things I had found and said I thought the priests were disgusting with what they were doing. I went on and on then I *'heard'* *'look at his eyes'*. As I talked his face was changing, also the colour of his eyes, at one point they were very blue and then brown.

The colour of his aura changed from white to black to brown. Then I stopped talking. He looked right at me. He was so angry – "you look at your own shortcomings." I was *'told'* not to say it, but I thought (my shortcomings are nothing compared to you lot!)

I found myself laughing at him then I got up and walked away. I thought now that was a bit of a different confession.

I felt this man was going to ask questions about me. I felt some fear but it did not last. I overheard one man say, "I do not want to go to this priest. I have my own spiritual adviser."

I told him, "Go your own way," with that we walked out.

I talked to the man, he said he worked for the poor but he did not agree with what was going on within the Church. He said he would not work with the priests or the brothers.

I told him that I was disgusted with what I saw going on here.

"Why don't you do something?" I said.

"Who would listen?" he answered.

I asked, "Have you talked to Mother Teresa?"

"Yes, but her hands are tied. They all know what is going on but no one does anything. The people that did in the past were treated badly. Some good aid workers were not allowed to come back to India."

"Well," I said, "I am opening my mouth."

"Be very careful," he said. We parted saying we would see each other again. He gave me his name and address. A doctor told me he could feel a great presence with me in India.

I also felt a great presence with this man; he was there for the poor he had done this work for so long. He was tired and weary everything was staying the same, he said, "No change."

I laughed and said, "Things are going to change."

He smiled, "I hope so," he said.

I talked to a group of people today. They told me they were from a girls' orphanage. These girls were taken from there and placed on board ships for the men that came here from Western Countries. The men only knew to start with that the girls were clean and the men would not catch anything. It was not till later when all was over the priest came around to the men with a hat for money. The men were later told to keep their mouths shut about this.

I talked to men who had been on these ships. They told me, "Yes this is the truth."

The skipper had told them there would be women coming on board.

They told me some were very young and they were physically sick when the priest came around with his hat. Some never went to church again, never bothered with it after this. Some said, "Don't let the wives know!" The men normally only talked about this amongst themselves.

But what these men did not know I found out as I spoke to the women that had babies by these men. All stayed in an orphanage until old age. No one wanted the women as they had children so they had to stay in the orphanage and work all their lives. Some kept their babies and left the convent (escaped) and had a dreadful struggle bringing the children up. These children

92

now know there father was British or Irish. Others in the orphanage had their babies taken away from them.

The men I spoke to about this told me they never got over it, when they found out what was really going on. They told me later in life it got worse for them - the shock of it all. The sad thing is as I spoke to some, they told me if they 'believed'₃ when they started out, they certainly did not now.

They all remembered being told to keep quiet about this. They said they were ashamed.

We would all like to think our grandfather, father, brother or uncle did not do this but they did. Some even raped the beautiful Indian women.

Notes

The picture at the front of the chapter is of an Indian church being done up (upgraded).

1. Duck feathers came from pulling them off live birds for quilts and pillows.

2. Back home in Cornwall I had to have lots of antibiotics to clear it. I think and know just how lucky I was. My doctor was on holiday and another doctor was standing in. He said, "The rats had given me a dose," as he looked at my legs. I had lots of fleabites and was lucky I had the good fleas not the ones that carry the plague.

3. 'Believed' or supported the Church.

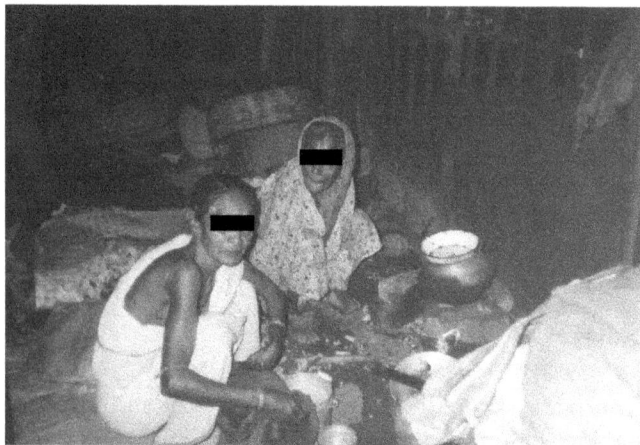

Chapter 8
Christmas December 1994

I was going to be at Mother Teresa's convent for Christmas. I was looking forward to it. We had been going around people's houses and chapels singing hymns. It was lovely. Then I saw a beautiful white and amber light. It was like thick smoke as it got to me.

I was *'told'* I was not to be at Mother Teresa's convent for Christmas, it would be a circus of people and cameras. I was *'told'* I was to spend Christmas with a lovely family and the whole picture came up in front of me of the family I was to be with, the orphans and children.

I later told Mother Teresa this. She seemed to understand. She told the orphans with a smile, you have a new auntie now.

I later found out they had TV cameras at Mother Teresa's Convent. It was flashed all around the world and I was *'told'* this was not right. But she had no say in it.

I was taken to a home run by the Church to look around. I was shocked at what I saw. People were in rooms with nothing and had no clothes on. They had lumps growing all over their bodies' small and big, even on their feet. Some people, men and women were walking around on all fours, could not stand up straight. They were like dogs. It frightened me as we came from the rooms to outside. There was a circle, as I went to go to my left to walk around, I was *'told'* go to the right. As I walked I saw people with so much disfigurement it frightened me to death. Some had heads like frogs, some missing limbs and some blind and in a dreadful state.

Some did not know where they were or who they were. I could see the people showing me this were also very disturbed.

We left feeling dreadful.

"What's going on," I said. "How come the people are like this?"

But no one would say anything. Later when walking along the street a man came towards me from behind a stall. He was tall; I noticed him as he was quite big and had a beautiful peaceful aura. He gave me a stone. "This is for you," he said, "you will come to know what it means in time."

"Thank you," I said; shocked at being given this. I went to pay him.

"No, no," he said, "it is for you."

Again I smiled and said thank you and went on as I looked at the stone, I had no idea what he meant or what the stone meant. It was a crystal with one stone on top of the other one square one being pointed on top.

I walked further on and just in front of me. I looked at a small old man sitting by a wall with a stick in his hand. Orange clothes around him, his aura was so wide, he put his hand up and waved me to him.

As I bent down he said, "The colours around you are beautiful."

I said, "So are yours."

He smiled and said, "You have the ability to be in your own country and here at the same time."

I was taken aback, I knew this, but how did he know?

"Yes," I said. "I know this is true." Maybe I needed to be told, the Indians knew all about this but my friends and I just thought I was a queer sod. I said, thanks to him and went on my way. Now I wished I had talked more to him.

I was taken down lanes and we came to huge places with gates and walls of about ten feet in height. On top of the walls were rolls of barbed wire. As we walked through the gates I noticed a lot of fruit laid out on the ground. As we walked further on there were men that looked like monkeys. They were on all fours and their backside was the same as a monkey - yet they were human.

I noticed a white energy go all around the man as he looked at me, I picked up his thoughts. 'Don't pity me, do something.'

I said, "I will," through thought form.

Then I was nodded to go another way. As we walked, I saw men with ears growing in their backs and the tops of their outer arm, I knew what it was but I had to ask.

"Is that an ear growing there?"

"Yes," I was told and then I was told we had to leave. I got the impression if we did not leave now someone would see us and then there would be trouble. We left quickly. Then I was told, "They experiment here."

"Experiment?" I said.

"Yes," they said, "like the Germans did."

(Oh my God!) I thought, "Can't you do anything about it?"

"Tell someone? Who will listen," he said, "it has gone on for centuries."

I did this when I got back to England in 1994 - talked.

All the talks I did were free but the people used to make a collection and the money went into the appeal. When I got so much, I would be told who to send it too. I went straight to the person with no middlemen.

I wrote to all the charities. I wrote to Blue Peter. I wrote to priests but only got prayer cards back from them telling me not to judge.

I wrote to the United Nations and got letters back about all their field workers and by the year 2000 they would have hundreds more.

I was buying some things from a little stall in a street in Calcutta when I saw a big cloud of purple smoke. It was changing and all of a sudden a man was beside me. I looked at the trader and wondered what had happened.

He said, "Hello sister." He told the trader he had charged me too much. "She has come to help you, charge the right price."

I knew this man was charging me too much but I did not mind. I knew they were poor, but I was *'told'* wrong was on both our sides. The stallholder for charging me too much and me for not saying so, *'be fair'* I was *'told'*.

Then I was *'told'* to buy milk for the babies on the pavement. As I did this I was *'told'* to let another woman give it out and I was *'told'* to watch her. As I gave her the milk and told her who to give it to, she did not walk, she ran to give the milk out to the Mams and she looked light and lighter. As she did this her aura shined.

Next I was *'told'* to give her money, to give to people. As I did this she said, "You want me to give to them?"

"Yes," I said.

Again she ran to hand it out. She was glowing and I was *'told'* she was an orphan herself. Then a man came over to us with his hand held out, he was dressed in rags. I was *'told'* not to give him anything. He followed us around. My friend with me kept looking at me so I just said I have no more money. She opened her purse and gave him something.

As he walked away, I was *'told'* look back as I did he was jumping up in the air laughing. I was shown a vision of him in a suit with money, yet he had taken money from an orphan who needed her money!

Two days before I left Calcutta I was *'told'* to go to a church, one I had been to before. As I set off, I did not remember the way. As I stopped I saw 'rose' coloured lights. I was *'told'* to follow; as I did I got to the church.

As I got inside there was just one person cleaning. I was *'told'* to walk around, I did. I did not recognise the statues, only the one of Our Lady.

I asked, "What am I looking for?"

I was *'told'* again, look around. As I walked around looking everywhere, I was *'told'* look down. As I did I was standing on a gravestone and my maiden name was on it. I could not believe it "Was I here before?" I asked aloud.

'Yes.' I was *'told'*. I always knew there was something about my name. I did not know what.

The next day I told my friend and I came back to take a photo of it. We had a taxi back and I was *'told'* as we stopped in traffic to give the taxi driver some money.

With that a young boy stood by the window, he wanted money. The boy just did not look right. Then all of a sudden, I felt an overwhelming feeling.

I was outside looking at myself inside the car but it was another time, a different car and I was with my same friend.

She was working for me. The taxi man, my driver and my friend were afraid of me.

I was in a lovely suit, it was in the 1930's and I would not give the little boy anything. I could see myself telling him to go away.

I could see my friend was disgusted with me. The next minute I was back in my body and the little boy was not at the window. I was *'told'* the Indian woman was with me before her birth had chosen to help me. I could feel something between us. I felt so close to her. The little boy was the driver and the traffic jam had been caused by a strike. He took me to where I needed to go.

Notes

The picture at the front of the chapter is of some of the poor that The Traveller helps.

Chapter 9
Coming Home

I was so shocked by all I had seen. I was in a right state at the end of my time in India. I was glad to be going home; I could not wait to get on to the plane.

I was having trouble with my eyes. I had a job to see at the time but when I got to the Calcutta Airport I was given a leaflet to fill out. I could not see any of the writing. I tried so hard to see it, even with my glasses but they did not help. I could not understand it.

I began to worry. I looked around then I was *'told'* to go to the man at the desk. As I got to him, he had a big smile on his face. I said, "Can you help me with this please? I cannot see it," and then I said, "I forgot my glasses."

He took it and filled it out, he was great. He pointed to where I had to sign and off I went. I could not understand why I could not see it.

Then it was time to get onto the plane. I had very little to carry as I had left everything behind. As I got on the plane I had a seat by the window. I had just sat down and a man was in front of me.

"What would you like to drink?" he said.

I was very disorientated. I was thinking tea, he said, "Whisky or brandy?"

Straightaway, I *'heard'* quite loud *'whisky'*.

I said, "Whisky please." I remember thinking I do not drink, certainly not whisky.

"Would you like anything with it?"

I thought, (sandwich).

He said, "Water and ice?" I was told, "No, no."

I thought to myself (he must think I'm a right wally$_1$!)

He went away, smiling. Then I thought, 'he has not asked anyone else if they want a drink' and still people were getting on the plane.

The man came back with a large whisky. I was *'told'* to drink it right down.

I did this - it took my breath away! I felt warm and my head began to spin. I put my head back and closed my eyes. I heard 'well done!' but I felt dreadful. I can't explain how I felt.

When I arrived at London Airport, I could not see what the signs read — they were a blur. I was thinking it was like this in India.

I followed a group of people. As I was walking through the airport I saw lots of people then I heard a voice I knew shout, "Mum!"

I looked around it was my son. I wanted to burst out crying and hug him but I saw the look on his face. I knew I must have looked dreadful - I felt it.

I talked to him for a while and then I heard a voice say, "Mum we are here too."

I looked to the left and saw my daughter. I put my hand on her.

"Oh! I am so sorry. I did not see you."

She said, "Mandy is here too."

She was at the other side of my son, his girlfriend, whom I liked very much, but I could not see her either.

I said, "I am sorry," again.

My son said, "Come on let's go and have a drink "

I could only see one face at a time, like a pinhole.

We sat at the table and had tea. This was such a surprise. I was not expecting to see them and had not spoken to them since. I left for India but I knew something was wrong with my eyes.

'Why could I not see?' I could only see a group of people, my eyes burned. My eyes and hearing had always been very good. I gave them the little presents I had brought them back from India and then I was going for the coach back to Cornwall.

They worked and lived near London. As I was leaving them, my son said, "Mum don't look in the mirror for a while and don't go back there."

I smiled, as they put me on the coach. I cried all the way back home thinking of the poor children and people I had left behind.

I was *'told'* I had to talk, talk and talk.

I went all over the place talking of what was going on. Some wanted to hear the truth, some did not. Some walked out.

I remember one lady after the talk apologized for me; she said, "You should have seen her before she went to India, she was full of life, so happy."

Another lady told me she could see, I was reliving it all over again in my face, (and I was).

Some of my so called Catholic friends who had known me over thirty years, crossed over to the other side of the street when they saw me coming. They would not believe all this was going on. I rang my mam and gave her hell for bringing us into the Catholic Church.

At one talk in a women's house, the big front room was full of people. As I talked I was *'told'* to look at the three women sitting on the couch. As I talked I could see three spiritual forms, then they bent their head in shame. I was *'told'* – *'they were part of it all at one time'*.

One woman sitting at the end of the couch got up, she looked at me and I picked up, 'no,' she thought, 'I am not going to talk to you'.

I was *'told'* – *'she is still not hearing or seeing. Her eyes and ears are still closed'*. I could see the other two ladies were thinking it. I had stirred up a lot of emotions within them. As I went on to talk, two more Church ladies got up and went. One, by the window,

101

took a diary out and started talking between them about what they had to do at church.

I was *'told'* they too wouldn't listen. *'Their so-called duties are more important than hearing the truth'*. The lady of the house apologized for them when I had finished.

I said, "It did not matter to me."

When they were looking at the photos of myself and Mother Teresa one actually said, "Is that Mother Teresa?" These photos were so clear. Her friend said, "Yes, it is."

I was *'told'* to say nothing.

There was no escape for them.

I was home just a few days and I was *'told'* to talk, talk and talk of what was going on – *'the truth'*. It went into the local paper that I was not pleased with the Church. Then I had a call, 'Could I give a talk in Truro?'

"Yes," I said.

The first place was a Catholic Church – a Mother Teresa group. Before all the people came, I told the two leaders of the groups the things that were going on, the abuse and the sexual abuse. I went on and on.

One woman got up and walked away. I was *'told'* to follow her and tell her more - I did.

Then she said, "You won't be able to tell the group all this."

"Why not?" I said, "It is the truth. They should hear it then it is up to them what they decide to do."

She was thinking then she said, "I was talking to Bishop X one day and he said when Mother Teresa dies, this will all come to an end." Then she said, "No - you can't talk of this."

I was shocked, "Well, what can I talk about then?" I said. With that, I was *'told'* – *'talk of the visions'*. "Oh no!" I said, "I do not want to talk about that." Even though I had talked to one of the women about it before. I remember telling her some things, long, long before I ever went to India. I told her I would write a book about it all and she said she would help me. So I did speak about the visions and some things about India and showed the photos of the poverty.

I talked to a lady that went to Calcutta over twenty years ago to help the Mother Teresa Convent. She said it was going on then. She said she was helping the children in the home for a while then one day the priest at this place wanted to have sex with her. She put up a fight so he threw her in an old out house and locked it. She was there for a time, nothing to eat or drink. Then one of the other aid workers came looking for her. He took her to the hospital. Her stomach was all swollen.

The hospital tried to tell her she was pregnant. She insisted she did not let him touch her. The hospital knows it goes on and of course it was malnutrition with her.

She got away thanks to another aid worker but what of the others and if they do this to aid workers, think what they are doing to the Indian orphan girls.

I asked her, "Why didn't you tell anyone?"

"Who would believe you?" She said, "Mother Teresa's priests doing this."

If I had not told her of what was going on now, she would not have told me.

I talked to nuns who told me and put it in writing that nuns are killed by their superiors if they don't support their injustices.

***

[Below is an unedited typed extract written from a handwritten letter by one of the nuns mentioned by The Traveller]

According to me a woman has her identity and dare do things that helps her. So keep up that integrity. A separation from the partner or even divorce will be a necessary on that path. Hope you are able to manage the risk and challenge of it. In India very few women dare it, even if she dies in the hands of the cruel husbands. I support your decision and think of you with affection.

I am fine and happy. I stick to 'Life Natural' and the part-time job. I have not told Sister R that we correspond. I am trying for a passport. I hope to go abroad, earn some money to buy a house and continue my service of people too.

I may not get anything from my family. By next year I complete a graduate course in Naturopathy and will be back to normal health. Being brought up in the convent style I miss a neat room and all its conveniences, although I took it upon myself. Now the stable of Bethlehem is so real. I stay with a family and when I have nothing and no one to belong to, everything is with humility. No sight to speak or act, even if it is a hut, it has to be one's own. I accept and no regrets of the past. The almighty upholds me with her victorious right hand.

In India nuns are killed by their superiors if they don't support their injustice.

Your photo of the aura is wonderful. The power is within God's spirit is living over us.
Love and prayers

Sister M

[Below is a letter from another nun retyped from the original handwritten one.]

Dear Traveller

I am very happy to receive your letter. I knew you would surely reply to me. I received your letter on the 20th of February. On the 20th of February I went to church to hear the Station of the Cross. When I came back from church to my surprise I received an envelope. I found your name written on it. I was very happy to receive a beautiful card, a nice letter, a snap and the twenty pounds. Thank you Traveller for everything you sent us.

Traveller you are very lucky because you took out a snap with Mother Teresa, very less person get a chance to go and take out a snap or can go to visit her. It was God's wish that you took a snap with her. My husband said to frame your snap with Mother Teresa and keep it in our house as a remembrance. I showed your snap to my relatives, they said how pretty she is.

A friend is good
A friend is kind
A friend like you
Is hard to find.

Red ship
Blue ship
But the best ship
Is friendship

From an Indian friend

* * *

Then I talked to a Calcutta born man, living in England. He told me it has been going on and on all the time with most of the priests. He told me, the nuns have babies too and I found it hard to believe.

I asked him why haven't you talked to someone about it? "Who to talk too?" he said, "who would believe you? The world had built a 'don't touch' to her, so what can you do but it is not only her organisation - it is all of them." Sadly I came to find out this was true for myself.

Then a good friend of mine died. He lived up country but was coming home for a service at the Catholic Church and to be buried. He and his brother had been so good to my brother and me when we had come here from Ireland so I wanted to go to the service, even though I did not want to go to this church ever again. I felt so angry towards it. I wanted to smash all the windows. When I came home I was driving out to do it and was '*told*' quite loud: 'NO! I am dealing with it,' but I was not listening. I kept going. I was going to get a stone and smash all the windows. As I got to the gate again I was '*told*' loud and clear '*Stop!*'

I was '*told*' to write to the Pope. I heard nothing back, so friends wrote on my behalf. One had a reply!

The day came for the funeral. I got to the Church. Just inside the side door I was talking to his family when the priest came out. I had not seen him since I had asked him to put a poster up on the notice board about going to India. He spotted me and came over to me.

"Hello Traveller!" he said. "I should have told you to come back and see me," he said.

"I did," I said. I did comeback and gave the letter and talked to Fr P but he was more interested in the bishop coming and seeing that everything in the church was ok for him. He took the letter and put it in his pocket. My voice was rising. He took my arm and led me into the front entrance. "Now look Traveller, you must not bring shame on your Mother Church. We don't want to hear this or see any of this in the papers, radio and hairdresser's shops or talks any more. You must keep quiet about all this. We will get you help."

I felt something going from my feet to my head. "Me! Bring shame on you! You are a shame in the eyes of God." Then I was going to tell him of the experiments and I *'heard'* *'No! I was not to tell him that!'*

Then I was *'told'* to tell him, *'now you look inside of yourself'*. "God said, look inside yourself." He looked shocked.

So did I, when I looked up the coffin was at the main door and the bearers standing beside us, hearing all. I was so engrossed with all that was going on in India. He also was in shock. We did not see the people beside us. I had never spoken to a priest like that before. I had stood up for myself and spoke the truth. I then walked over to the family and the group of marines. When I saw Kris$_2$ (who had died) standing in front of me, he looked and felt lovely, so peaceful. He told me not to worry about him - keep talking!

During the service, the priest tipped most of the Holy water over the coffin. His hand was shaking so much. He wanted to talk to me after the burial but I headed off in the other direction.

I heard later he was ringing up to see what I was saying at the talks.

I was *'told'* I had created a hornet's nest.

I thanked the people for what they had done.

Then I was *'told'* to go to Ireland. I was to talk to the people there. The local paper also put in an article about the Church money not going to the people. I talked to a lot of the people and friends and told them what was going on.

I was in the town one day and was *'told'* to go into a restaurant for tea. As I entered I saw there were ten money boxes on the counter chained together so no one would run away with them. The owner was there and I was to tell her the people abroad do not get this money. "Well you surprise me now," she said. "I find that hard to believe."

"Well it is the truth," I said as I sat down to have my tea.

I went back into the restaurant two years later, the boxes still on the counter. That place is closed now it is a clothes shop.

Then I was *'told'* to go to the courthouse and wait.

Ask about a house₃. I was *'told'* as I got inside. Yes, there was a box for the poor Indians and it mentioned the place in India I had been there too, the place where I had seen people coming and asking for something to eat but they were being turned away. As I was standing in the hallway this day, a woman came for something to eat. So she was given a little food, very little but only because I was there, I was told later.

So I told the man in the courthouse, "You know I have just come back from India and I can assure you, the people do not get one penny of this money."

"Now that does not surprise me," he said.

"Really?" I said, "well it surprised me." I could not believe it. I went on to talk about a house and as I was leaving, he asked; "Do you want the money in this box for the people? Take it."

"No thanks," I said, "but thank you." I went back two years later, the box had gone. Great stuff I thought, they are listening. At one point I was so worried, that people did not believe me as though I was lying. As if anyone could lie about a thing like this?

Then with this beautiful light, I was *'told'* – *'you are not held responsible for what other people think or do. You are only responsible for telling what you found, what you saw and heard!'* I felt a lot better after that and kept on talking.

Notes

The picture at the front of the chapter is of the Cornish flag.

1. 'Wally' – this is slang for a stupid person.
2. Name changed for privacy.
3. A place in India, the name being changed to protect people living there.

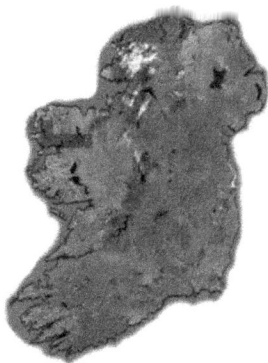

Chapter 10
Ireland

I was *'told'* to go into another shop. They too had money boxes. I told them the same as I bought a newspaper and chocolate.

"Do you know," the women behind the counter said, "the priest pulls up outside in his big car comes in empties the boxes, jumps into the car and drives off. Most of the time he does not even say hello and we have being wondering about all this."

I was *'told'* to do this in a lot of shops, pubs and restaurants, I did.

Then one day my sister said, "We will go to Cornell's Court, in Bray, to do a bit of shopping. It is nice there."

Off we went. We were trying on clothes. I had a lovely linen jacket. As I put it on I could see a huge big spider going up around my shoulder. I started to shout, I got so worked up, my sister and another woman came to me. "There is a spider on me!" I shouted, as I was trying to take the jacket off.

I was jumping around, "There are no spiders in here," the woman said.

My sister explained to the women she has just come back from a hot country with lots of insects around and she is still uptight, as I got the jacket off.

I was in a terrible state of fear, as they shook the jacket; a huge spider fell off and onto the floor.

"Oh my God!" the women said, "Look at that. It must have come in with the drivers."

That was the end of the shopping trip. I realized just how bad I was. Before I went to India, I was never afraid of spiders but this trip had brought everything back to the forefront, the abuse as a child I had to face up to and what had happened to me.

No one knew in my family. I kept it all quiet, as did a lot of children as they are doing now in India. Then I was *'told'* I was to tell one of my sisters.

Oh! I did not want to do this. I was also afraid she would not believe me. As we went in for a tea, I picked up the courage and told her, she believed me.

Then the strangest thing of all I was *'told'* I had to tell my first husband. Oh! I felt great fear I said, I did not want to do this again. I was *'told'* to tell him. Then I said, "I do not know where he is." I have not seen him in years. Then I thought (is he here in Ireland and I will bump into him somewhere?)

Well over the days here in Ireland this was my last day. I would be leaving in the morning 6:00 am. I had seen a nativity set in a shop window a few days earlier. It was in the sale and was a good price but I still would not get it. It would have been nice for Christmas. I decided to go and get it before the shop closed.

Off I went down the street just coming to the shop, I was *'told'* – *'look to your left,* **the car***'*, as I did my first husband's brother was looking at me. We talked about my trip to India and seeing Mother Teresa. He could not believe it.

Then I asked, "Where is Paddy now? I would like to speak to him." He gave me his address and phone number.

When I got back to Cornwall one day I was *'told'* to ring him now. I got the number and dialled. My heart was pounding, I thought, I wouldn't be able to say it. I wanted to put the phone down, yet I could not. Then, the voice said, "Hello …Paddy."

I said, "Yes; it's The Traveller. Did Kris₁ tell you he gave me your phone number…" and we went on to talk about India then.

He said, "What do you want Traveller?"

"Oh Gosh, I do not know how to tell you this but I think you should know." There was a silence for a while, I wanted to put the phone down again but then I thought I'd have to ring again to tell him, so I did it there and then.

I said, "The reason the marriage was not consummated was I had been abused as a child and the fear I had was terrible."

I heard his body sigh; everything had fallen into place now.

He said, "Traveller, I felt such relief I could not believe it."

Then I was *'told'* – *'he needed to hear it'*. We went on to talk a long time after that and he phoned me a few times. He wanted to meet me to talk (not for sex, he said) but to talk. I thought that was lovely.

I talked about India and my experiences there for two years, and then in 1996 I had a letter passed on to me from a different part of India. 'Could I get water to pay for a pump to be set up in a village?' Straight away I was *'told'* loud and clear I had to do this, there were more things I had to *"see"*.

I was to go to India again with the money. Oh! I didn't really want to go. I thought I had seen it all, what more is there to see? I was *'told'* again I had to go.

I started to raise money one more time. In the meantime I asked about prices. I phoned South West Water in Plymouth (UK), they were very good and sent me all the details I needed.

I did not like asking for help again as this was not going to the Catholic Church or Mother Teresa but I was *'told'* - *'the money would come in'*.

Some people stopped me in the street and gave me money. People wrote and asked me what they could do. Others sent me cards with money in them but with no name or address. One saying, "May God go with you!"

Someone stopped me and said, "The Holy Spirit told me to give you this," and handed me money. I also worked nights and mornings to raise money. I worked at aromatherapy, reflexology and I also did healing. I never took money for giving healing; I always did it for nothing. But now people left money for India. This also happened to my Mammy; people left her money for me.

Then it was time to go.

This time, just like the first time, before I went to India, I received visions of people I could trust. One lady had her black hair over her left shoulder and she was wearing a light pink sari. There was also a man with a mark on his face and a young boy with a bound Hindi turban on his head. I also saw a young man with a huge red aura around him and a man with a blazing white aura around him.

I heard on 'Five Alive' a nine month old baby was given milk and cheese, he choked on it and but was resuscitated. I was *'told'* - *you do not give a baby cheese it is much too heavy. Their insides cannot take it.* It will cause problems, mashed or not, it would not digest.

Notes

The picture at the front of the chapter is of Ireland.

1   Name changed.

Chapter 11

Bombay

The time had come to collect the money from the appeal and exchange it for a cheque. I was putting it all in one name, but as I went to do this I was *'told'* quite clear, just £1,000 in the man's name, the rest was to be in travellers cheques. So I did this. Again I was *'told'* – *'the coach and plane will be a safe journey'*.

The morning came to travel. This time I had to go to a different part of India. I was to fly to Bombay. Again I was *'told'* – *'Don't worry'* on the coach taking us to the airport. I was *'told'* – *'Look to your left and right out the window'*. As I did, I saw lovely big, round lights, bright as bright can be. I had seen this on my first trip in the plane to Calcutta. When in bad weather it was like fine gold string going from one light to the other as if bringing the plane safely to the ground.

I had written to an Indian man I met for a short time while in Cornwall, he said to let him know if I was coming to India. Then as we stopped for a rest for a short while I was *'told'* to phone him to see if he could meet me at the airport. As I arrived at Bombay I went to enquire about accommodation. I did not know if the man could meet me or not, and yet I could get a room not far away for 20, 30 or 40 rupees. I told the man if no one is here to meet me, I will be back. I went to look outside the airport. As in India the people are not allowed inside and have to wait outside. The men are there with rifle guns on their arms to make sure everyone stays in their place. It is a bit frightening. I remember in Calcutta my friend was coming in with me to the airport and a rifle came down in front of her, she was told, "Go back!"

I was outside looking for the man through the crowds of people. I saw my name held up but I did not recognise the man. We both said, "Hello."

"My God, you look completely different from when I last saw you!" I said.

He said: "I am in my own country now and laughed."

He had booked me into a hotel; it was the only one he could get me into, as everywhere else was packed.

As we drove off along the streets the poverty was dreadful and it seemed to be hotter here than in Calcutta. I had a job to breath. As we arrived at the hotel, it was huge, all lit up and two doormen all dressed up with turbans.

(Oh) I thought (I don't want to stay here. I will go and get a cheaper place).

I was *'told'* I had to stay here; there were things I had to see. The room had everything - TV, phone, fruit and drinks in a fridge. I had changed some of my travel cheques. I had my money separate from the appeal money. We paid for the room.

The man took a huge bundle of Rupees and handed it to the rep. I could not believe it, all this money?

As I asked the price they just looked at each other and smiled. People were paying with huge stacks of Rupees. I thought this is a far cry from the poor.

I left my things in the room and we went to the other airport to see about a flight for me to travel the next day. We went out to look around, on the way back I again was *'told'* – *'watch and listen'*.

114

A little way on some children came running up to us, one little girl asked for something to eat. As I was going to give her some money I was told by the man "Put your money away." If you give to them you might as well throw it away," and he said something in Indian to the children and pushed the little girl back with his left arm.

I got back to the hotel; there was a wedding going on with music and dancing. The bride and groom were being carried and people were pining money on them. Then I was told, you can go home and not talk of the poor anymore. He laughed, it was a well to do wedding. It was a nice feeling standing amongst the people. Back in the hotel room I put on the TV, but I was told to walk around the hotel.

As I walked around there was a lot of white people. The white men were all dressed well; as I sat with a drink I was *'told'* to watch. I saw white men (older men) going into hotel rooms with young Indian boys. For a minute I thought: the Indian boys were working for the men.

An hour or so later I watched the Indian boys come out of the hotel some looking very frightened. They were putting money in their pockets, then the penny dropped, they were being used for sex. A hotel door opened and a policeman came out with his truncheon in his hand slapping it into his other hand. A few seconds later out came this little Indian boy, he was only about six-eight he looked so frightened. He had been beaten. He came out behind the policeman and ran down the stairs. The policeman had a smile on his face with his truncheon banging from one hand to the other.

I was *'told'* to stay and keep looking at the policeman. I did this till he was out of sight. I went back to my room I felt sick.

(What a bloody disgrace this is), I thought. White men coming here for sex and police hurting innocent little children; who were only getting a few rupees to help them live. The problems they are going to have later in life, the hurt and pain they are going through now. I could see it on their little faces. As I looked around, no one was taking any notice and this is the norm - that's the sad thing!

Next morning I went downstairs for breakfast but I did not really want it, so instead I went out into the garden. It was so hot. There was a big swimming pool with people sitting all around it. In one corner there was a huge big table with lots of drinks and fruits on.

Seven young waiters were taking the drinks around to the people. On another corner there was a group playing, the music was lovely. I was *'told'* – *'sit down'*, as I went to a sun chair the waiter came and asked if I wanted something to eat or drink. I asked if I could have a glass of water, he looked surprised.

As I drank the water, I was *'told'* - 'look to your right'. There was a white man on his own, lying on a sun bed, in his 40's or early 50's. He finished his drink, then held up his hand clicking his fingers, a waiter ran over. They talked, the white man not lifting his head to look at the waiter. I watched as the waiter picked the empty glass up from the ground, leave and come back with another drink and putting it back on the ground. The white man did not even lift his head to say thanks.

He did this all morning, clicking his fingers for a drink or for something to eat. I felt ashamed to be white. These white men were all different nationalities. Then I was *'told'* to look at the young boy, way over, sitting under a tree. I was *'told'* again, *'no one will notice, go over and talk to him'*. As I walked over and sat beside him I learned he was working at the hotel laying marble slabs. He was working on an extension to the hotel and had come out from the dust.

He was white with dust, as I looked behind him I could see his workmates. They also had all this white dust on them. Then I noticed his hands were in a dreadful state - all cut. He had rubber finger gloves on. As I saw them I could not help thinking of the young men working on the churches with their fingers bleeding. So I asked: "Can I see your fingers?"

He looked at me for a minute then I heard a voice say, *'Show her your fingers'*. But there was no one there, I could not see anyone, then the boy started to take his finger gloves off.

I could see the pain on his face as he was trying to get them off. I wanted to tell him to stop but I knew I had to see them and yes, they were swollen, cut and bleeding.

I was *'told'* to give him 500 Rupees. As I did this the boy looked very surprised. Then he was getting up, "Where are you going?" I said, "back to work?"

No, he was going to follow me.

I thought, (No, no) I said, "I was told the money is to help you and your family."

With that the boy said, "Thank you!"

I walked away quickly and got another drink. I sat down for a while and looked over at the men working. Then I got up, waved to them and walked away. I put my glass back on the table and said, "Thanks," to the waiters. They were just standing in the heat waiting to serve some horrible people. Then I was *'told'* – *'they are here for sex'*.

I went off to look around. I was being picked up at 2.00pm to go to the airport. I was *'told'* he would be late, so then I sat in the hotel lobby with a fruit drink. I watched again as the men went into their hotel rooms with young boys. Then the man came to pick me up.

As I set out for the airport, I could not get the young boys out of my mind. I asked God to help them. Going into the airport the man said he could not stay, he had to get back. I said, "That is ok. I'm alright."

He was telling me where to sit and where to go. There were a lot of people here. Then I saw a giant, tall aura of energy. It was coming towards a man sitting opposite to me on my right, as it got to the man I saw a big purple circle colour. It was like a hoola hoop, it went right down over the man and through the chair. Then another aura came, a little smaller coloured ring went over the man, as it got half way down, the man was standing on his feet and walking to us. Then another ring went over him, he said to the man I was with, "Can I help?"

They exchanged cards stating who they were; "I will look after you," he said, "I am going on the same flight". He asked, "Where

117

are you going?" and said he lived not far away and he would take me.

"Thank you," I said. I had not seen this man in visions but seeing the colours that came over him, I knew he was ok. The man I was with left me but the plane was delayed. The man asked me to look after his bag; he went off for a while. I must say; I did get a bit worried. He had been gone a good while. Then back he came and held out his hand. He had got me a bar of chocolate fruit and nut. "Thank you," I said, as I went to eat it. I offered him some, he only had one square, as he had sugar diabetes but was ok.

We got called to go through to the plane. Then we got stopped. This happened three times.

As we walked and got on the plane I saw the big round lights again and was *'told'* – *'all is well'*. When the plane landed it was so smooth the people on the plane cheered and clapped.

When we got off several hours late, he told me his driver would be waiting but we were so late the airport at Calcutta was told the flight had been cancelled. So when we got to Calcutta there were no staff to get our bags, they had gone home. We had to wait again. It was after midnight now.

The man said, "You will have to come home with me, we have not long moved, so we haven't much furniture but we have a spare bed."

I said I was not worried about the furniture. Then we got our bags. All the workmen had big smiles on their faces. I felt as if I was in Ireland, everyone was so friendly and no more troubles. We were all talking, the men talking about the flight. Then off we went to get a taxi and drove to his house. I tried to pay for the taxi but the man would not take my money, he paid for it.

He had to knock, knock and bang on the door to get in.

The light came on, the door was open, but the shuttered gates in front were locked. I could not believe it when I saw the woman coming down the steps, it was the one I had seen in the vision, with black hair hanging over her left shoulder and wearing pink, exactly the same as I had seen her. I knew everything was all right.

She was surprised to see me, yet not surprised. They talked; he explained about the flight being delayed, she said they were told it was cancelled. The woman gave us cold drinks and she showed me to my bed. I felt great warmth.

Here I went to bed while they stayed up and talked. There was no mosquito net, so I just threw my net over myself, not hanging it up. I put the sheet over my head, woke up next morning and my nose was red and swollen with bites. The husband was up and gone to work the wife and I talked and went for a walk. She showed me photos of her son, his wife and children that live in America.

The people here all rise three or four in the morning, pray and then get breakfast; they are full of energy, needing little sleep. I loved it, when I was there I felt so fit and ate very little.

It was time to leave. As I put my bag in the rickshaw, the woman was talking to the driver. I was *'told'* to leave 900 rupees, I put 1,000 on the table and left. I thanked her at the rickshaw, she told me to come back any time.

I got to my next place to stay I was going to find out about the trains, times and prices to go to South India. Then I was *'told'* *'no!'* I was not to do this. I was to talk to a person I had meet when I first came to India. So I went off to talk to them and told them what I was going to do. Straight away he said, "Michael has just come back from that area, he will go with you, he will find out about everything." He shouted the name, out came this young man from behind a curtain, it was the same boy I had seen in the vision with the really red aura around him. I was *'told'* – *'he was really angry and in time he will tell you the reason'*. We talked and he said he would come with me and that I should not go alone.

Then I was *'told'* to take Philip, another boy I met when I first came to India, with me.

Well it was an eye opener, they had to bribe with money to get the tickets. I stayed out of the way so they could not see me. When they got the tickets I showed myself to give names. They were surprised that I knew about their scam, (the tickets were one way) as I was not *'told'* what day to come back. I only knew it would be before 19th December. As we went to the station to get the train, we were told the train would be late. I sat down.

The boys went to walk around. Suddenly I started to sink down. My body jolted. Then I just started to get very, very hot. I began to sweat, I felt as if my whole body was on fire. I felt as if I was travelling, but I was sitting on a seat.

The boys came back and asked if I was all right.

"Yes," I said.

It felt as if I had lots and lots of coats or blankets on me and each one was being taken off. It must have lasted for an hour. I could not think what was happening to me, as I wiped the sweat off my face the sinking feeling stopped. I looked around the station. The boys got me a bottle of water to drink then they said, "The train is in."

As I got up from the seat I felt dreadful. My trousers were wet and stuck to me as I walked. I wanted to look back, but was too afraid. I was sure if I looked at the seat I would see myself still sitting on it. As the boys looked for our names on the sheet of paper pinned to the train we got on.

Then I was *'told'* - *'look out of the window!'* as I did I was relieved to see the seat was empty. As we started the train journey that lasted two days and one night. I began to feel different. I felt so happy. We were into the journey only a few hours when I got up and walked to the doorway. I sat with my feet stretched out, just looking at the scenery.

The train was travelling slowly. As I sat I thought I have done this before. Then I saw myself as a young boy pulling two white cows and the bell in the middle. I was a young Indian boy. I had seen this before but did not know what it meant. As I travelled further I saw scenes I had seen as a young child in Ireland, when my mam and doctor thought that I was sick and delirious. And here I was in this hot country I saw as a child over forty years ago, sitting on a train.

I could hardly breathe as I saw the vision as a child. Here I was - doing it. I felt so excited! As the train stopped we got out and walked around for a while before climbing on again. While sitting in the doorway of the train, we were passing lots of people who had a sheep or a cow grazing. They were a long way off in the distance but looked so peaceful.

Next I was *'told'* – *'take money and throw it out!'*

"But the people are too far away," I said. I was *'told'* - *'they will be guided towards the money so throw it out'*. So I took Rupees out, scrunched them in my hands and threw them on the ground when I had done this I was *'told'* to stop. I was *'told'* to keep looking, I watched as some people started to walk towards the track.

The train stopped. I was again *'told'* to buy some nuts from the young boy who was by the window. A few seconds later, a young lad stopped nearby. His aura was lovely, I was *'told'* to give him fifty rupees (equivalent to £1). The nuts were just a couple of rupees. I gave him the fifty rupees.

"Oh!" he said, "I have no change for this."

I said, "I do not want any change. You are to keep it."

"No, no," he said, "you wait." He went off and a few minutes later came back, just as the train was pulling off. He had a little box and three sweets in it one for me and each of the boys. The boys with me told him to keep the money.

He said, "Thanks," and jumped off with a big smile on his face.

As we reached our destination no one was expecting us and was surprised. As we got to the village we were taken to the owner of the orphanage. While at the orphanage I found people working in the paddy fields and getting very little money for this.

They had a monsoon while I was staying there and as I was taken among the paddy fields talking to the people. I found that they were buyers, saying it was damaged with rain. The people could do nothing. I was *'told'* to give money to all the boys just to it take out. I gave money to all the boys working there. I told them it was to help them and their families. This is what I was *'told'* to do and not to count the money, just hand it to the boys.

As I was leaving, walking back through the fields I was *'told'* to *'look back'*, as I did I could hear one of the boys saying, "Give me the money." He was going around to each of the boys and taking the money I had given them.

I asked, "What's going on here? That money was for the people to help them and their families." I started to shout at the man who was with me. I was so angry. I said, "I have found this everywhere I went, the poor people are getting no help it's taken off them!"

(So here I was, a paddy having a paddy in a paddy field. I laughed latter, but not at the time).

I shouted, screamed and wanted to know what was going on. I would not move 'till I found out. I could see the Indian people were so afraid and shocked at me talking to their elders like this. It is not done here.

He went off; one woman put her head in her hands talking to herself. Then he came back to me it's the son of the owner of the field, he was only taking it and going to give it back later.

The boy was beside him I told him, "He is lying, I don't believe it!" I walked away from the fields. We went back to the village.

A little while later I was talking to children. When I was 'told' – 'look to your right - Here he is!' From around the corner, this young man came towards me, his aura was big and white, it moved quickly around him. As he got to me he said, "I'll be your eyes and your ears." Here we shook hands and he told me his name. He was just as I had seen him in a vision.

Next day I was taken to hide behind some trees and bushes. An aid agency was giving out food to people that had been in the floods. The TV cameras were there, all the food was given to the people. Later, when the cameras had gone, the food was taken away from the people. I could do nothing but watch.

I was taken to a small Indian village where they had nothing, their little mud huts had been long washed away by the flood water. An old man in his 70's, in his mud hut, one side of it all washed away. Three families lived in it. I watched as aid workers came to look at all the damage. Nine men in a group I heard them say we have a lot to do with the aid money get the workers in the rice field to help you build it up. Get them all to work here and they went off - the village did not even get one rupee.

Priests are calling the people animals and inhuman until they are baptized as Catholic. They even put this in writing in their paperwork going to the western world to get money in. the only ones I found inhuman were the priests. I felt sorry for the decent men who are in this organization. They should now come out and talk about it.

Then I was taking to another small village about land. This village was Catholic. The priest had told the people to give the land to the church for their sins and the sins of their ancestors. I also had found this in other parts of India. Priests were taking land from the people, a lot of people told me they would be able to support these whole families and villages with food, if they still had their land they could have been rich by now (farmers are killing themselves over these matters). But the poor are depending on other people for food. I went to one mud hut and I was *'told'* - they are all the same; four little bricks for a fire, one string bed (single) where all the family sleep. When the children are older, they are on the floor, where there are rats and all sorts of insects crawling around. As we walked around I saw no electric, no water and no toilets.

Then I saw a young boy in a group of children. I was *'told'* to ask about him; as I pointed him out, the man with me called him to us with his hand. The boy came over. I was told his mam had died, his father could not afford to keep the eight children they went to the priest for help, but no help was given. So one day, when the boy came home he found his dad hanging. The boy had not spoken since. So the grandma was looking after them. Then I was *'told'* to give him money, so I did this.

I told him to pay to see a doctor and give his granny money to help her (looking at her she had little to eat). As we walked away again I was *'told'*, - *'look around'*, as I did I saw the money being taken off him by a man. I started to shout again, but my throat was sore. I could hardly speak from when I had shouted in the paddy field. I later found out this man was a government official and did not live in the village but had his own house and was well off, but the people were afraid of him.

I went up to him and took the money out of his hand and gave it back to the boy. I said, "Don't take that from him! God told me to turn around to see what you did."

He spoke in Indian to the boy. The boy went away, later he came back with his granny. I could have cried, she could hardly see. She was worn out. I felt so sad and angry at the same time to see what was going on here. The granny had brought the money back to the government official to give it back! I told her it was to help her. He told her to keep it and go. He was a pig just like the priests I had met.

Then as I walked on, I saw children eating what I thought were Holy Communion wafers. I did not say anything. I thought I was seeing things and went on. I was asked into a house for a drink. I saw bags of Holy Communion. I asked, "Is that Holy Communion?"

"Yes," I was told, "We make it here," as he handed me a handful.

"You make it here?" I said. (I was shocked).

"Yes, it's rice paper". There was plain white for one church, white with a splash of red on it for other places. I was looking with my mouth wide open. They must have seen the shock on my face, "Oh! It is all right," the man said. "It's only holy when it is blessed." This is being made in a place where people have no food, water or sanitation. The Catholic Church is fleecing them.

All their food is going to the western world that has plenty. If that was not shock enough I was taken to a place where food was being sent from the western countries all old and out of date. Some of the food even had maggots in it. A man cut a little carton of drink and in the bottom were maggots. The Indians told me it's too old for the westerners to eat; they send it out to us. There was also a stock of old second hand clothes that were only fit for the bin. I was disgusted. When I got home I told one of the charities. One charity worker told me: "Well if they are that poor they should be glad of anything!" The Indians are very loyal. I was *'told'* – *'be loyal to the right things'.*

I talked to the nuns of a village who had asked one of the Irish charities for water and had been refused. They were told to ask someone else.

At another village I was *'told'* of the priests' sexual and physical abuse. How they work the people after taking their land, how they have to build churches, chapels and convents, yet still no water, electricity or sanitation. Well, nothing for the poor people. Yet it was their land. Now the people are poor, the Church rich. They are doing one thing and preaching another.

One day I was *'told'* to go to mass. As I did the priest came in to say mass. I was *'told'* he will look at his watch within twenty minutes. I looked at the time and yes he did, fifteen minutes had gone and he looked at this watch. I was *'told'* - *'they are just going through the motions'*. Women were on one side of the church, the men on the other. The priest looked at me and turned away (he felt uneasy).

The people told me when the missionaries came with their prayer books we had land. Now we have the prayer books and the missionaries have our land.

Next day, we went on to another village, the rain had been terrible. The roads were like rivers. One bus had turned over. You had to know where you were going here. As we got to the village we had a job to get the auto rickshaw through the muddy lanes, they were stuck. Then I was *'told'* to watch, as some Indian men came to help us push the rickshaw. I watched as the white energy went around them I was *'told'* – *'look at their feet'* as they pushed. The veins in their legs and feet came up but their strength was unbelievable. The rickshaw was free. I thanked them and we went on a bit further and stopped. It was too muddy; we went the rest of the way on foot, leaving sacks of rice in the rickshaw.

The same thing as with other villages the people had nothing. They had lost most of their crops. They had to eat by the rains. They said the rains seem to be getting worse. There are no drains for the water. So the people have to walk around in it until it soaks away. The people were picking berries and leaves to eat.

We went to the rice mills and brought back sacks of rice. All the people with children filled up their containers and little bags with rice in them. They were divided up and there was no way I was going to take photos of this. The people were really hungry. The children's little bellies were swollen. I was not going to take photos of this just to show the western world (the white people).

In this area the churches were all being painted and done up inside and out. I saw churches that we call 'listed buildings' that were in a bad state of repair were being rebuilt brick for brick both outside and inside. It was the same inside with painting and electrics. Again the people were told there is no money to help you, that the money has only come in for the churches to be built or done up. They were told the money had come in from donations.

Next day I was taken to a church that was being done up. It was being built like in Lourdes, France and again a story that happened over 100 years ago of a ship at sea. The ship and all the people perished but a statue of Our Lady floated to the water's edge so the man who owned all the land gave it to the Church.

Just lately they built a six feet brick wall all around the church, stopping the local people from grazing their sheep. The people pulled some of the bricks down to let the sheep in. Now the church is taking them to court. In the same area a local trader had a stall outside the wall of the church and the Clergy will not have it. They are also taking the traders to court to stop them going anywhere near the walls of the church. I found the traders not harming anyone.

The people have just a few pots and pans most lived in mud huts with sack or banana leaf roofs. If they have no string beds to get them off the ground away from all the insects, rats, etc. then they lie on raffia mats. They walk for miles with a clay urn full with water. They wash, bath and do jobs in the rivers and on the fields. They have no tap water, electricity or toilets.

The women work in the building of roads and some of them carrying huge stone rocks. If they work more they sometimes, get a little extra money, one or two rupees a day, if they are lucky. They get fifty pence working from dawn to dark and still have to give a dowry when getting married.

Then I was taken to yet another huge church, not only inside but outside. People had to climb a huge hill on which there were huge statues of the 'Stations of the Cross'. The hill was very steep and half way up there was holy water for people to take or wash in.

I was told many, many old people and little children have fallen to their death on these hills and were told by a priest, "It's ok, they were doing it for God."

Then I was taken to St. Vicente de Paul. (I know this) I thought; people who helped the poor, only here they were not helping! I was *'told'* – *'They stopped many years ago and give very little'*. I also found out it was a big organisation making and selling all the things for a church, such as statues and challises. Western people collect money, give it to the priests it goes back into the church for all the statues.

I also spoke to priests and nuns who had left the church. They told me they did not like what was going on. It takes a long time for a priest to get permission to leave but a nun can get released in about three to four months. They hope they would get a lump sum of money as they left. The nun explained to me they were told when leaving the Church they had to leave everything they had behind. That you leave with little. The Church said, 'We have clothed, fed and educated you, when sick, we had medical bills'.

So they left with little. They all told me here poverty started when they left the Church. They had the security of the four walls, but they told me they never knew what it was like to feel like a woman to do as a woman does. To look at yourself as a woman, they all told me it was hard. They did not for one-minute regret leaving the Church but they are only now - living.

I also found India was like Ireland years ago when a lot of boys and girls went into the Church to be nuns and priests. If anyone came out of the convent or clergy, they would be looked down on. Their family would feel they had turned their backs on God. Not for one minute thinking the Church was wrong. The

127

same is happening in India. If the son or daughter leaves the church some families won't talk or have anything to do with them again.

There is a lot of unrest. I spoke to lots of nuns that would like to come out but are afraid to. They said it has nothing to do with God, but you don't know this until you are in it. I remember talking to two men from Ireland that came out from the priesthood. After a short while one told me he was afraid of his life to go to sleep. Other priests would come in and try and get into his bed. He told me still today I have not told my mum or dad why I left. I told him the time has come now to tell them the truth. People do get a calling to God but you don't have to be a priest or a nun to do it.

Then one day we were going to get a bus. I was going to see an area of land where there are pepper, fruit and spice trees.

I was *'told'* - *'the bus will not come'*. We stood for ages. Then we went to another place to stand and wait again. I was *'told'* again – *'the bus would not come'*. I had a job to believe this, as there are busses all the time here.

It was so hot, I said, "We will get a drink". As we walked away from the bus stop I was told by the women, "Maybe it is just as well the bus did not come. We don't feel safe on the busses now. People who have Aids are so angry. They are on the busses stabbing people with their needles."

I said, "Oh! You should have said. We will go and see it in a rickshaw. It's better."

In one Church it was so dark. I looked around. There were lots of big windows.

I said to the person I was with, "Does it look dark in here to you?"

"No" she said.

Yet, as we walked around it seemed to be getting darker. Then, just below the alter there were lovely flowers. They had lots of light around them. I was *'told'* - *'The children have put them there. All the children are innocent'*. As we left the church, just outside the door, I was *'told'* - *'look back at the big doors'*. They were wide open and there was an old lady lighting a candle. All around her was light and whatever she was praying for, she was most sincere. I saw a white mist rise up from her head. That was the only light in the church I was *'told'*, all the rest was black.

I will never forget it. As we walked away I was *'told'* – *'look back'*. As I did I saw a man sitting on a board hanging with two ropes painting the outside of this big church.

Then I watched as orphans from the orphanage (Catholic girls) lined up and marched to the big churches to clean them on a Saturday. I saw about 30 young girls doing this. They also have to give up their beds if visitors come. The girls sleep on the floor.

I was travelling to a village with some people. I was told to watch the boy. As the journey went on the boy looked lighter and became happier. His aura was getting brighter and brighter. As we arrived at the village he went to run off to someone, he was shining. Then his mam said, "Don't get dirty." The boy's colour$_1$ dropped a little. He was thinking of his clothes but he kept running off. Later the boy came back with a man and boy. There was something between them. (But what?) I thought. (What could it be? Why were their auras shining so brightly?)

Then it was time to leave. When we got back I noticed the boy's aura was fading the further we got away from the village. I didn't want to say anything in front of the boy but I did ask him, "Would you like to live in that village?"

"Yes!" he said, his face beaming as he was telling me.

Then to my surprise the father later said to me he is not our son, he belongs to the man you saw him with on the bike. He is family and asked us when he was very young could we take him. We would give him a better life and we could educate him, the boy doesn't know yet we haven't told him and he asked me not to say anything. I said I would never do that. But as I was *'told'* the spirit knew he was going back home.

Businessmen, as well government officials, set up orphanages and sponsorship deals for children in the poor villages. The sad thing is their mammies and children know nothing about it and the people get nothing. The orphanages or homes and sponsorships are set up in the wives names. But the men do it all. It's just a front.

I saw TV, videos, plates and mugs still in boxes sent in or bought while in India at the owners of these organisations own homes.

If anyone comes to look around the children are brought in from poor villages, afraid to say anything. It's all a front for the visitor. If it's their birthday the visitor will even get a cake. While the poor still go hungry. I know money is coming in from America, Australia, Ireland and other countries.

One man's wife couldn't have children. So with the money that was coming in to help the poor he used it for IVF treatment for his wife in hospital stays. The poor did not see one penny and the wife went through hell.

When the poor came for help, the person that was receiving the aid money for the poor told them 'pray to God for help' and gave them nothing.

I said to him, "You do the same!"

"What you say, what you say… pardon me?" He said.

"How does it feel to have it said to you?"

I found when in India, antique dealers, some from London came and bought lots of things and then sell them in London for large amounts of money and giving the people in India very little. The same thing is happening with larger companies.

Then I was 'told' – 'Mother Teresa needs help', she was sick and in hospital. I was 'told' – 'sit on the bed'. As I did this I was out of my body and standing at Mother Teresa's head. I was looking down on her in the hospital bed I was 'told' to put my hand at her head, holding it. Then I was back in my body on the bed. I later talked to the nuns, they told me Mother Teresa has had electric shock treatment.

I later spoke to other people that had had electric treatment. I thought all that had stopped,

Then I spoke to a doctor and asked about Mother Teresa. I was told it was touch and go for a while. She was not responding to treatment. But she is a little better now. As we talked I saw a light go all around the doctor's whole body. Then the doctor said, talking about Mother Teresa's convent.

"It is the mafia that is in there."

"The mafia!" I said. I was told that before. I knew something was going on, when I talked to Mother in 1994, she just referred to them as 'they'. I said, "Who are 'they'? Is it the church priests?"

She looked at me, she looked so sad and just put her hand on my wrist and said, "Come and pray."

Then Mother Teresa was back in the convent and one day I was *'told'* to go and see her. I was also *'told'* the time. So off I went. It was mid-morning and I was *'told'* there will be a mass for her now. She was not well enough for the early one. I was *'told'* – *'stay for mass'*.

I went into her chapel and with that Mother Teresa was wheeled in. In the wheel chair she had her blue cardigan on. I was *'told'* – *'go to her and hold her hand'*. As I got to her with my hand out, Sister N (her successor) pushed her way to me and caught my arm with her hand and pushed me back.

She held my arm tightly. I said, "God asked me to come here today, now, and to see Mother".

"Yes, yes," she said and we are trying to keep her alive.

With that mother called her back, smiled at me and called me over. She caught hold of my hand, "Are you staying for mass?"

"Yes! If I can," I said.

"You stay," she said.

There were not too many people there. Some aid workers, and some nuns. It was not as packed as the early mass, but a lot did not know of this mass. The priest saying mass walked slowly to the Holy Communion. They walked down to give Mother Teresa her communion.

Then I was *'told'* I was to go and take it too. I would not go. The priest was putting it back and all of a sudden I found myself at the alter saying, "Can I have communion please?"

He looked at me. I said, "I am a catholic." He did not like it.

So he unlocked and took it out. As he was giving it to me I saw a huge white aura around him. The communion looked so big and I thought I would never get it into my mouth. Then I saw a figure and I was told you will not ever have to take communion again. (On my 1998 trip I found out why I did not need it). With that the light faded but I did not know what it meant.

As I walked back I looked at Mother Teresa and she smiled at me. I thought if Mother Teresa was not there I think the priest might have refused me. I know he did not like me going up and asking. I had the communion after Mother Teresa. That was the last time I took communion. Mother Teresa asked me to come back the next day.

I did but she was not well again, she was sick in bed, so I said I would come again another day.

As I was leaving I was 'told' to listen, as I did one nun was poking a man in the chest. He had his money and passport taken (stolen) and he had come to ask for help. He told the nun, "I will pay all back to you."

"Yes, yes," she said, "you and thousands more come to knock on the door."

The nun's aura was very dark, yet the man was telling the truth and felt terrible. All he wanted was a little help. As I was leaving she set off for the office and got some paper for him to write on.

Then one morning I was 'told' to go and see Mother Teresa. As I got to the convent Sister B told me, "She is not seeing anyone, she is really poorly."

"Alright," I said, but then I was 'told' – 'Sit and watch'. I said to the nun, I would just sit here a while. She 'looked daggers' at me.

As I watched nuns coming and going I watched people coming in to see Mother Teresa. The nun told them all as she told me, "Not today," and then she looked at me. With that more people came in to see Mother Teresa. One couple with a girl of about ten to twelve asked for their daughter to see Mother Teresa.

"No," she said. The man sat down, took out his chequebook and wrote a cheque. The nun took it straight away and took the little girl in to Mother, to her sick bed.

I was *'told'* – *'This happens often!'*

I was going to go but I was *'told'* to stay. A man came in and sat beside me. His aura was very dark.

He looked at me; "Why are you waiting, go away and think of Mother Teresa."

I just looked blank at him, as if I did not understand him. Then a medical person, who was looking after Mother Teresa, came out.

"Ah!" she said, "Hello Father." He got up and took out a jewellery case, like a necklace or bracelet in length and handed it to the woman.

She opened it and looked at him he said, "This is for you for helping Mother Teresa."

"Oh! I thank you very much. It is so beautiful, but I cannot accept it."

He put it back in his pocket they talked for a while and then both left.

In came another man and sat beside me. He had a camera.

I asked, "Are you a photographer?"

"Yes," he said, "I have come to take a photo of Mother Teresa and her doctor."

I asked him, "Do you take photos of the poor?" I told him what I had seen.

"I know," he said, "I see that every day but people don't want to see it, they would rather see a photo of Mother Teresa or any other celebrity."

I was *'told'* – *'it is true'*.

Then a nun came out, "I am sorry," she said to the photographer. "Mother is not well enough, to have a photo taken."

He left. I was then *'told'* to leave, but to come back later.

I was leaving that evening.

Later in the afternoon I was *'told'* to go and see Mother Teresa but to take Mary with me. I could not understand why I had to take Mary. I asked her to come. Oh she was so delighted.

"Me! - see Mother Teresa. They will not let me in."

"Yes, they (the nuns) will," I said, as I walked in the door, Mary behind me.

The nun on the door smiled.

I said, "Hello."

Then she tried to stop Mary.

I said, "She is with me."

She was allowed in and we sat on the bench.

We were there for a short time talking, then I was out of my body.₂ I was standing beside Mother Teresa's bed. I was helping her up. I was walking behind her. I saw Mary and myself still sitting on the bench.

Then there were American volunteers helping her. (I needed Mary to get me back into my body with a bang). The experience was just like when I had to put my hand on Frank's leg. I could see him outside of his body looking at himself. He knew I was there, yet he was fast asleep then.

I knew no more until Mary banged my arm and told me, "Look! Look! Mother Teresa," I found myself back in the physical body.

As I looked up she sat beside me. She was smiling. I wished her goodbye and gave her a hug. I put my head on her shoulder.

Again I was *'told'* – *'put your hand on her back'*. I did and then I held her hand.

"Will you come back?"

"Yes," I said.

She asked, "You have a camera?"

"Yes," I said. But I was not bothered about a photo. This was just fine for me. She told Mary to take a photo.

As Mary was taking it, she asked again, "Will you come back?"

I laughed and looked at Mary.

I left for the airport.

Checking in I was *'told'* to go and stand behind a man and a girl. The man was full of tattoos, including his head.

134

As I stood behind him we got talking. I just happened to say, "I hope I have enough money to pay for the taxes."

He said, "I don't think you have to pay that anymore, it is in the tickets."

"Oh!" I said, "I had to pay before."

"Well, don't you worry," he said. "I have money and I will pay it for you." He was there with his daughter at a Buddhist temple he said he was a Hell's Angel once.

We talked about all sorts of things. We stopped over one night, to break the journey. At this hotel they wanted to see our passports. When the two men were looking at mine they said, "Ah! Gerry Adam's country."

I smiled and said, "Yes, Ireland."

They said to each other, "Put her in room."

That worried me.

"Travelling on your own?" they said.

"Yes," I said. But I felt safer than in Calcutta. At least I was on my way home.

Later at London Airport I met the man's wife and granddaughter, while waiting for the coach travelling home.

Notes

The photograph at the front of the chapter is of a rice paddy field in India.

Indian Hotels

All the hotels have electric and water for people but the villages or towns close by have nothing.

1.   'Colour' in this context refers to the boy's aura.

2.   Out of the body experiences are sometimes referred to as 'astral' projection, the 'etheric' or spiritual body. In all cases it is a body which is separate and yet still connected to the physical. The Traveller has the ability to utilise such a body or bodies in waking consciousness. There are many documented cases in

hospitals of near death experiences where another conscious body seems separated from the physical and left staring down at it from above the bed.

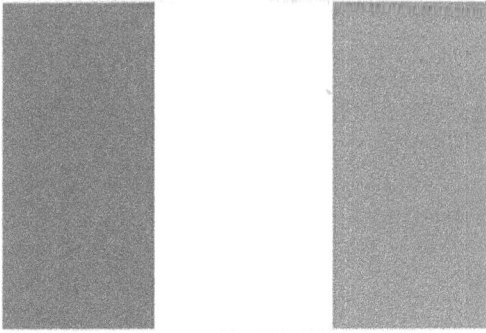

Chapter 12
Return to Ireland

On the 24-2-98 I was *'told'* I had to go to Ireland this day to Dublin.

I was *'told'* I was to take it all to the 'Archbishop's Doorstep'.

So I would have to fly. The flight was for 10:40am but it was late. We left 11:20am and it was a lovely day and a good flight, even though it was a small plane.

We arrived at 12:35pm I saw a figure in front of me as I got off the plane, there was red all around it like lights. It was a cloudy day as I got to the bus station. On the bus I was talking to a lady coming back from a holiday in England. She was loaded down with bags. I asked if I could help her and we talked. She was from Mullingar. I was *'told'* to tell her where I was going and some of what it was all about. She wished me luck.

At the bus station I was *'told'* – *'go there now'*. So I left my bag in left luggage and looked at the busses going to Dromcondra. I knew this address as I had been there before and I couldn't help thinking as I walked up the drive, the horrible way they had treated me when I had to come here about my annulment. They

137

were disgusting! What they asked and said to me in the 60's. Of course I couldn't say anything at that time about the abuse. I even had to make two trips back from England to talk to them. On the last trip to see them I spat on the ground and said to my friend, "I hate this fecking place!"

I rang the bell there was a speaker on the side of the wall. I had to say what I wanted.

I said, "I have come from England to see the bishop."

"Have you an appointment?"

"No," I said.

"Well you should have made one."

"Can I see you or someone and talk to them please?"

"What's it about?"

"I'll tell you when I see you."

A man came to the door. He asked what I wanted.

I said again, "Can I see the bishop?"

"The bishop is a very busy man, you should have made an appointment," he said again.

Again I was 'told' – 'ask to see the bishop'. I asked again and was told again, "He is very busy and he is not here."

I asked, "What's his name?" He told me with a smile on his face.

"Can I help?" I was 'told' to tell him. I did tell him but he never moved. I asked, "Did you know all this?" He never answered.

I said, "You all know what's going on." Then I told him Mother Teresa was afraid of her life of you, I talked with her.

He looked at me.

I said, "I'm ashamed of my life of you." I told him, "I'm writing a book about it all!"

"Where do you live in England?"

I was told not to tell him. So I said, "London area."

"Have you got a pen and paper?"

I was 'told' again, 'No'. So he wrote the bishops name and phone number on some paper and gave it to me. "Phone here tomorrow," he said.

As I was leaving he said, "Are you still a Catholic?"

I looked at him, "Would you be if you had seen all of this?"

He looked at me and I walked away but then I turned around and said, "Tell the bishop when you see him, he should be sorting out his own house first before talking to others."

As I got back to the station I looked at the bus times. But then I was told to go to the bed and breakfast where I had stayed before and the girl got me the phone number for the right station.

I walked and asked if the girl was there.

"She is at her break," I was told.

"I'll only be a minute," I said.

So I was taken to her. She had had her hair cut - it was long before.

I told her I was writing a book and also talked about the incident at the bishop's door step. She was eating with other girls as I told her this. She explained that her mum and dad had had trouble with the Church; one was Catholic the other Protestant. She wished me luck.

As I got back to the bus station I had time for a drink. I went into the restaurant and was 'told' – 'look who's here!' I looked around and there sitting, having a cup of tea, was my mam and sister. They were in Dublin for a day's shopping. They didn't know I was coming home.

My sister was looking at me thinking, 'It can't be - The Traveller?'

I went over to them laughing.

"Oh my God!" my sister said, "it is you!"

As I sat down, I said to my mam, "Where do you think I've been?" She looked at me, as I told her what happened she was very worried.

I said, "Don't worry they don't know who I am. I never said."

But they were fearful. I could see their auras. Then she said, "Get a cup of tea there…"

As I went I saw pancakes. I took one of these with my tea. I said to my mam, "There are pancakes there!"

"Well … it's Shrove Tuesday." I didn't know. My head was in such a state.

Of course the next day was Ash Wednesday (25th February 1998).

Imagine my surprise when I was *'told'* – *'this time you are to go and see the parish priest'* (from my hometown).

Walking through the large gates, looking at this lovely big house and all the beautiful shrubs and flowers I was *'told'* not to touch him.

How could I do this? People usually shake hands. I held my bag in front of me with both hands. After I rang the bell I was there for a few minutes before he came to the door.

The door opened, "Hello," I said, "could I talk to you for a few minutes.

"Yes. Come in and sit in there, I am on the phone."

As I sat looking around I was thinking, (I hope he doesn't shake my hand when he comes in).

He came in and sat down next to me.

"Now, what can I do for you, is it marriage? A Christening or …"

I stopped him smiling. "Nothing like that," I said.

"What's your name, I do not remember seeing you here before?"

I was told not to tell him my name yet.

I said, "I'll tell you my name later. Then I carried on telling him what I had to. I told him all about what I had found within the Church in India.

Then I was to tell him of the visions to which the Church used to beat me and make me kneel for hours to pray. I carried on talking, then I was *'told'* to tell him of the abuse, sexual abuse and that my marriage was never consummated. I was also *'told'* to tell him of the bishops and priests in Dublin. The awful things they said and telling me never to take the communion.

He was to hear a lot.

Then he said, "What is my aura like."

I was told to tell him, but not mention of the black coming in on his left side. So I told him what his aura was like – very grey, a muddy grey. I was *'told'* to screw up my face as I told him of his aura and to my surprise he said, "Is it black?"

140

So I said, "Not yet." Which it wasn't, but it was coming in.

Then he said, "I will help you if you want to take the abuse through the courts. We all have the facilities for that."

I was *'told'* tell him *'no, you are going down a different road'*.

As I was telling him this, a white line appeared on the wall. I was told this is the true road. Then a white line came from the first line up a little way and then branched off, it was not straight but very crooked. I was told this road is the Church. I was told to tell him this.

As I did I said the Church is wrong, they are not telling the people truths. To my surprise he said, "I know, but what can you do." Then he said, "Do you know the bible?"

I put my hand up in front of him, "Don't you quote the bible to me."

"No," he said, "in the garden of Gethsemane Jesus upturned the tables and said, 'Let my father's work be done'."

"Yes!" I said, "and it's God that's bringing you down."

"I know," he said. Then he told me of a friend of his who had been in the priesthood for over forty years and was up for sexual abuse.

I said, "God is bringing all the bad ones down." I told him, "I was only about seven to eight years old when I was told the convent was going to close and here over forty five years later it is closed. The nuns and priests told me this was the devil telling me this."

"Tell me … who are you?"

I was *'told'* tell him. I said, "I'm The Traveller child of Mary₁"

"As you talked," he said, "her name did come into my head. You are as charming as your mother to talk to."

I was *'told'* – *'he has never talked to your mum'*.

Then I was to tell him of the Charity 'Throka' in Dublin. I was also *'told'* – *'Tell him he should not charge to open doors or gates'*. I didn't know what that meant. I told him anyway.

"Cork₂ is not a poor town you know."

I said, "That's not the point! As well as nuns asking for help for their villages, especially water and being refused."

"Ah, ah," he said, "well you know who that is over and what has come out since."

I didn't know and didn't say anything. But I knew there was another person involved with it.

"Have you got a pen and paper?"

"No," I said straight away. I did not have to be *'told'*.

So he got up and wrote the name of the person and organisation and gave it to me and told me to go and see her but I was *'told' - "No!"*

As I got up to leave there was a knock on the door. A man was standing there. The priest said, "Oh hello Paddy. Did you find the ladder?"

I said, "Goodbye," and went out between them not touching him.

I was later *'told'* – *'he charges to open the main doors for a wedding.'* If people don't pay they come in the side door. Some months later I was *'told'* – *'he had a heart attack and was quite ill in hospital'.*

As I made my way back to the car behind some shops I was *'told' - 'there is your Mum'.* I looked up but didn't see her. Then, there she was, coming from the lane, a shortcut from the house to town. I was *'told'* – *'ask her'.* I said where I had been and told her what the parish priest had said.

"I never spoke to the man!" she said "and he has never spoken to me."

Again in 1998 the priests were telling lies and what I was being told was right. Only now I know the Church is wrong and what I was *'told'* was right.

Then I was *'told'* – *'everyone is in place for the big war between good and evil. Everything that has gone on behind closed doors will be out in the open. All things will come to light. There are people in the past that have said nothing but now they will awaken and be in the right place at the right time to take action'.*

I was told one Thursday morning – *'EXPOSE them to the world'.*

I was *'told'* to phone the number I got from the bishop's house in Dublin now. First I talked to the receptionist - a woman. I was *'told'* – *'ask her who she is working for, is it God or the organisation?'*

Then I was to tell her of the sweatshops and some other things. I asked her if she knew she said she didn't know and then said to me you are making me feel very guilty now.

I apologised and said you needed to know this. I said, "My money is running out."

"Give me your number, I will ring you back," she said. She did. She told me I will put you on to father B.

I talked to him of what I found and also what happened in the 60's to me at the bishop's house in Dublin. "Here?" he said. "YES," I said.

"Where are you are staying now?" I didn't answer.

Then I asked, "Did you know the Church owned all these things?"

No answer. I asked again. I felt so angry. I asked again.

"Did you know?"

"Yes," he admitted.

"Oh my God!" I said, "and is it true as another priest in England told me, you can't council me, as God has shown me too much.

He sounded deflated. "Yes, that is true," he said. "But I think you should talk to someone of the abuse and what happened here. Father O could talk to you."

"No thanks," I said, "I'm disgusted with all of you. Thanks for listening to me," and that was it.

How could I talk to them?

So that was it. I had done all I was *'told'* to do.

Notes

The picture at the front of this chapter is of the Irish flag.

Chapter 13
India – Hyderabad

I was *'told'* again that I had to go to India. This time I said, "I don't want to go!" I felt fear. Then I was *'told'* - *'Have no fear! There is more for you to see and hear'*.

I was *'told'* I was to go to a different part of India and *'told'* where to go, where to fly to and then again I was *'shown'* more people in visions, again that I could trust. I was also *'shown'* a vision of the young man I saw on my second trip. "He will guide you," I was *'told'*.

But I still didn't want to go. Over the weeks ahead I was working and talking about the third trip. I said I was going to help the people. But I couldn't understand how, I was feeling so afraid. I told my friend, "I don't feel right about this trip. Even though I was *'told'* - *'have no fear'*.

Then, one day I had just got home. I was only in the house a few minutes, when again a huge beautiful golden light told me, *'Do not be afraid – look!'*

144

I was shown a huge vision of my return with a green top and brown skirt on. I was smiling and looked happy. I felt a bit better after that. But still I wasn't 100 per cent. My insides just weren't right about this trip. I told my friend of the vision.

Well that will make you feel a bit better she said. Well right up to the day before I left, I still didn't feel right about this trip.

My friend told me the day before, "If you do not feel right about it do not go, we have *FREE WILL*.

I told her I don't understand it. All I do *know* is I will be ok. I still feel the 'ibygeebes', we laughed.

She wished me luck and said she would be praying for me.

Next day I set off on the coach.

Again just outside town I looked out the window and there was the lovely circle of light on my left and over on my right, I felt safe and then I knew I'd be ok.

I got to the airport and went to check in. I handed in my tickets.

The lady at the desk told me, "You are not booked in. You have not been put on the computer." She asked me to have a cup of tea while she sorted it out.

I said "Oh, it's ok if I haven't been booked I can go home and come back again another time." I went back after a while but she still hadn't sorted it all out. She told me to take a seat for a time and that she would call me.

So I thought I'd better ring home and leave a message that I might not be home for a while. My husband was there and I talked to him about it.

Each time I went to India I was *'told'* what to do and who to go with. This time I was *'told'* to get the tickets on the TV. I had done it all ok and paid, but as before when I rang$_1$ around the seats were all gone. No one could get me out the day I wanted to leave, every seat was booked.

Then she called me, "We have spoken to Crystal and all is fine. Now would you like a window seat?"

"Yes," I said, "Non-smoking."

As I got on the plane there were plenty of empty seats. I spoke to the stewards; there were two Irish girls on it. I told them I had a job to get a seat. They told me everything was booked. Yes we heard this from another person. We get this all the time.

"But why," I said.

"I don't know," she replied.

We talked about India. She said I was very brave to go alone. I remembered thinking, (I'm not alone!) I was also thinking (I won't be seeing Mother Teresa this time) and that made me sad.

I got on well with her. I liked to see her laugh.

Well it was time to get off the plane. But I had not seen anyone to talk to, as I'd been shown in the vision.

Walking around the airport I spotted the blue trouser patterns, turned up trousers and the black boots with a buckle on the side. That's all I saw in the vision from the bottom of the leg and feet. I went to ask her about India. She was an Indian girl.

As we talked we just 'clicked'. I had to get a doll for a girl in India and she came and got one with me. We walked around, talked about everything. I was *'told'* to fly to Bombay but I was to go to another place – Hyderabad. So I tried to see if I could get a flight to Hyderabad, but all the flights were booked, so I had to go to Bombay, as I was *'told'* to see this women and her family from Bombay. She was living in London with some of her family but her sister had cancer and she was going to see her. She hated travelling on her own, and as we got to the bus outside the airport her aura became very, very dark. As we sat down she began to shake.

I couldn't believe it, this was her country, why was she like this? I caught hold of her hand and arm. I said, "You are ok. You will be fine." As I put my hand up on her shoulder and back, I said again, "You are ok."

After a while she calmed down.

"Oh, I am sorry," she said, "I get panic attacks."

As she was in this attack her aura was very black and getting smaller (shrunk) it also cracked.

So we both needed each other. She said she would love to have come on the journey with me, but maybe another time.

We exchanged addresses and she asked me to come and stay with them some time. She said they were vegetarian but I could have whatever I liked to eat. She felt like an old friend. Then I was *'told'* we were together in another life.

As we arrived at the station to find out about buses to Hyderbad and for her to go her way a policeman came over to me while she was inside. He asked me if I wanted to rest and that he knew an air-conditioned hotel room. I was surprised. I said, "I'm not tired," as she came out she shouted at him, "What did you say to her? Go away."

He was gone. She asked what he had said to me and I told her. It never dawned on me it was all about the sex trade. This was her own countryman, yet she shouted at him, for me - a white woman she didn't know and had just met.

Then we had to go our different ways. She to her sister, me to a place I'd never been before. We bid each other goodbye and off we went.

I got on the bus - it was packed. I was the only white person on the bus. It was a long journey, very hot, but I was fine. I felt a great presence with me. I felt calm even though I did not know where I was going.

There had been a lot of rain. The fields were full of water, but the strange thing is no one sat beside me as we stopped and people got on. One man got off rather than sit beside me. That hurt, they just saw the colour of my skin. I saw them as I saw myself - a human being, a person.

I must say that it was only on this journey I found this.

As the journey ended I got off the bus and looked around.

Where do I go now? I thought. I was *'told'* to wait as men and boys came to me to carry my bags. I was told, stand and wait. Then this young boy came over to me, about 12-16 years old with the same aura and red/burgundy turban on his head I had seen in a vision. He just picked my bag up and off we went. He took me to a hotel. The outside looked terrible, not the paintwork but the aura! It was very dark, "Do I stay here?" I asked.

"Yes," I was told.

147

It felt weird at the front desk. I asked for a room. "Single," I said.

There was a man sitting behind me on the seat reading a paper. The man on the desk said, "I have two rooms, one room on the first floor and one on the third." With that I was out of my body watching the man reading the paper.

He told the man at the desk, making motions with his hands, to put me on the first one. Then a young boy appeared to show me to the room. This man sitting down also told him to show me to the first room. Then I was back in my body.

The man saying, "This room is best for you. How long do you want it for?"

"I don't know yet," I said, "I'm seeing some friends tomorrow and then I will know."

The boy took my bag with two keys in his hand. "I will show you the first one," he said.

Oh, the room was dreadful! Everything about it was horrible. It felt horrible! Then I was told to stay here. (Oh dear) I thought.

I said to the boy, "This room is ok thanks."

He asked if I wanted anything to eat.

"No thanks," I said.

He went off. I did not unpack anything; I did not want to lie on the bed. It was awful. I sat for a while then I felt very tired, so I lay on the bed with my clothes on. Just as I lay down I started to travel again. It was at such speed. I saw myself as a man in a German camp. I saw the men in German uniform. I smelt gas and the taste in my mouth. It was a horrible smell. I saw men pulling something out of my mouth. I had no teeth! I was struggling but they were holding me down. There was something in my mouth.

I watched them holding me down on the bed. Then I was back in the room, lying on the bed.

I sat up. I was so frightened. I felt my mouth and my teeth; my heart was jumping so fast. I went to check the door. It was still locked. I had seen myself in another lifetime.

I pushed a chair by the door. I did not want to sleep, but I did for a while. I was so glad to see the daylight. I felt my mouth again, checked my teeth. I did not wash and I did not want anything to eat.

I think I was still in shock. I felt a bit angry too, that this should have happened here. Then I walked outside with my address. There was a queue of auto rickshaw drivers. I was told which one to go to. I handed him the address.

"Can you take me please?" He looked around at the others. Then he went over to ask directions. Off we went. He was not on the main road but the back lanes. Oh the poverty as we went along, I thought, (I bet no one comes here with help). I saw no other white people. Some young children looked scared when they saw me, their eyes would open wide.

We reached our destination. All the children came running with us as we drove to the house. My friend came out on hearing the auto. Oh I was glad to see him. We went inside and met the family. This was the man who said 'I'll be your eyes and ears'. I told him where I had to go.

Straightaway he said, "I'll come with you."

Then he said, "Today is Sunday."

I said, "Is it Sunday?" I had lost track of the days and he had never been away before. But he took me all around the villages to see how the 'Direct Aid' project had helped.

As we got to a railway track we had to stop - a tram was coming. Then I was *told* to look. As the tram passed on the other side I saw a young boy in a green shirt. He was skipping towards us, singing away.

The man shouted to him. He looked so happy, his aura shinning, he came over to us, he told us he was going for messages for the village. Then my friend said that was one of the boys that was bought out of bondage (slave labour).

In some areas if the father falls sick they take the boy or girl to work. If a person borrows a little money and they can't afford to pay back then the children and wife sometimes are taken to work in paddy fields or sweat shops. Often the owners of the land or shops keep them and their Mothers or fathers don't see them again and it could be for just a few pounds of our money. But for the Indians earning so little they can never pay back and live. I didn't go to get the children because if they knew they had help the price would go up. I also spoke to men that would sell their blood or organs to get money to help their family. Families that have girls often can't afford dowries for them to marry and that causes problems.

I talked to people that pick the tea leaves and they had nothing. I was 'told' the tea goes out in big tea chests and then it's put in fancy packaging. I was given tea in brown bags to bring home. I was taken to another village and was 'told' just to hand them money. It was to help the children with schooling.

The people want their children to learn, to have a better life to know more. We travelled back for the hotel, going back a different way, my friend coming with me to see where I was, also to talk about the journey I had to take.

I was 'told' to give the auto driver a load of money. I took it out and asked if this was ok. As we got to the hotel I gave the driver the money and I said this is for you, and then I gave him the fare. He looked surprised, we said, "We will see you again," as he came into the hotel with me. The two men looked so surprised to see me with an Indian. We went up to the room, my friend said straight away you can't stay here it's terrible, get your bag we will check out and get you some other place. As we got to the desk my friend said, "She is checking out straightaway."

"Is the room not good? We have another one. I will show you."

The two men looked at each other, "Yes," the one said, reading the paper, lifting his head up from his paper.

"No," my friend said, "she is leaving."

We were told by one of the workers that some hotels pay young boys to be at bus and tram stops to bring people to them. Sometimes the boys do it just for food and shops also do this.

The worker told us of another hotel his friend worked at. I was 'told' – 'go there'. We did. It was much better. My friend went off, coming back in a few days. I was told which day to move on.

I was in the hotel room for about an hour and there was a knock on the door. As I opened it, standing there was a young man I had seen in a vision, right down to the chequered waistcoat and moustache. He asked if I needed anything.

I wanted to talk to him. So I ordered. He came back with the tray and we talked. He told me he would take me out the next day if I wanted to go and see his family and see a temple. The boy was poorly with sugar diabetes. As we got to his house he had to have an injection. His arm was so thin; one of the girls (worker) had to lift the flesh up on the top part of his arm to get the needle in.

They had three little girls who slept on mats under the bed on the floor. I found this a lot, at one point a doctor had a whole family of four live in the little space under his stairs and of course worked for him day and night when needed.

As we set off to get an auto rickshaw, he spotted his friend, an auto driver, to take us but said there was a strike on and the drivers can't go.

They talked and off we went. He took us all over. At one point, as they went into a shop to get a drink, I was *'told'* – *'look behind!'* As I did I saw a young boy about 10-12 years old, with one leg coming down the street hopping with the aid of an old stick. I was told to keep watching as the boy passed and just in front there was a flip-flop on the road, the boy looked around put his foot into the flip-flop and went off smiling (one shoe as he needed).

I found the same in this area. Churches being built, fees taken from the poor to marry as christens and give, give, give. They were not giving anything to the poor and the land was being taken off them.

Then it was time to go again. We got to another village and met a young woman who had written to all the papers and books for help. All the organisations passed the letter on and it was sent to a friend's group. He passed the letter to me. As I went to open it I was *'told'* I was to help. So I wrote back to the woman.

She told me of her village, her sister and a man that was helping them but they were so poor she thought she had to do something and so she wrote the letter to an advert she had seen in a paper saying they give help. But of course they didn't give help. They just passed the letter on and on until it got to me. Well I sent money for them to help buy a sewing machine.

We kept writing to each other. Then in 1998 I was told I was to go see them. When we did, I arrived on a Sunday again but did not know what day it was. The people again had all the crops ruined with the rain - they had nothing and the strange thing is the girl could not speak a word of English but we could communicate through telepathy₂.

She told me she was pregnant (she was married to the man who helped her and her sister). I was in a bank in the area and a man came in and deposited a lot of money in a fixed account for five years.

I found out this was the bishop's aid and he was doing this every week for the bishop. But if anyone goes to him for help they say no money is coming in, the people knew there was. I was to leave money here and not count it.

We went to a temple. I was *'told'* to leave my shoes on as we were walking in but everyone was taking theirs off. People were walking in their bare feet. As I walked I heard someone shouting, "Stop! Stop!"

As I looked around I spotted the man shouting. As I walked towards him he said, "Take your shoes off this is a Holy Place!"

This man's aura was so big, with a smile on his face as he took my shoes.

"Do you want me to walk around and show you everything? I think you do."

I was *'told'* – *'yes'*.

"Yes," I said, as he took us around this beautiful place, it felt familiar, yet I'd never been here before.

Then we got to this huge statue of a black bull. The workmanship in this building was fantastic.

I told him I have a great feeling about this place. The strange thing was before I went to India I had seen a vision of an Indian showing me a figure of a bull and feather carving to go around my neck. I later saw this and bought it and wore it to India.

As we travelled further we came to the temple itself. There were Buddhist priests there praying. A priest looked at us, came over and gave me a little bunch of white flowers and two bananas. I was to eat one banana, keep the skin and the other banana was to go with some flowers from my bunch and they were to be left at the temple.

By telepathy I could hear it all. Then with his silver tray with incense burning he put it in a circle in front of me saying something. I felt as if I wanted to give something and I was told there was no need, but I wanted too. There were a lot of people there, Indians and Westerners. I rolled the money up small and put it at the back of the tray. With that the man that took us around (telepathically said) see that - see what she did. Put it behind so no one could see and the priest said, "Yes."

Then he told me, "You have the ability to be in this country as well as your own at the same time."

"Yes I know," I said.

When we finished walking around he said, "You will be prayed for often."

"Thank you," I said.

As we were leaving I was going to throw the banana skin away but I was *'told'* I was to keep it with the flowers until they die. The flowers lasted for days.

Notes

The photograph at the front of the chapter is of where The Traveller was told to throw the banana skin into a small fire.

1. 'Rang' is slang for telephoned
2. 'Telepathy' is communicating mind to mind.

Chapter 14

Sai Baba

I visited a convent to see Sister P, a friend from another part of India. She was the one I had seen in a vision showing me the flower. I was *'told'* not to phone to say what day I was coming, although she had told me to phone her and let her know.

So I did what I was *'told'* - I did not phone. As I arrived at the door, a lovely girl opened it. I was *'told'* she would help me, (help me in what?) I thought.

I asked for the nun and she told me Sister P did not know what day you were coming and one of our girls was hurt so Sister R had to go on a trip (she was up north when I visited) but we will make you comfortable until she returns.

Over the days I met the other nuns – they were so young. I also met the nun who was supposed to go on this trip that Sister P went on. She told me that just as she was walking out the door she had gone flying (fell over) and broke a bone in her foot so she had to go and get an x-ray and plaster put on it and could not go. I was *'told'* it had to be like that. I was later to find out the Church was launching a campaign paying a lot of money out. But I found out the nuns and priests were going around to the poor villages asking and giving one thousand rupees (£20.00) for any girls coming into the convent and of course that is a lot of money to a poor family so they send the girls off. Sometimes two or three sisters or more are sent off, as they cannot afford a dowry for them to get married.

Then the girls are taken to a convent to be assessed and to teach and will then be taken to another part of India not seeing their families for years.

I talked to some women that this happened too. They said I remember so well when they came and took me away from my Mummy and daddy and she cried. They have been doing it for years and years. They said one lady was in her seventies.

One young Sister said to me I dreamed you would find me and take me away from here. I said if God wants me to find you I will, no matter where the convent sends you. They all asked me to pray for them. Their work is so hard and they have to put up with the abuse too – that's why they don't like it.

Then I was asked if I wanted to go to a home where a mother had died. I was *'told'* I was to go. As we got there, there was a huge crowd outside the house. I was the only white person there. I felt as if I was intruding but I was made welcome.

As I got to the room where the dead woman was there was a man taking photographs of the dead woman and her family then I was *'told'* – *'look'*. As I did the dead woman's spirit was standing behind the coffin looking down at herself and looking around she said she was at peace now, life was a struggle but she had fresh bunches of flowers in the coffin beside her.

Then I thought back to May$_1$, when I was *'told'* to give her the flowers. They had beautiful colours and smells as I put them on her coffin. I was *'told'* you will come to *know* what this means (I now *know*).

Later I saw the nun that took these poor girls to another convent. Her aura was so black, like black smoke moving off her and it felt and smelt terrible.

(Oh!) I thought, (if only you knew the damage you are doing to yourself and the poor children).

155

It was time to move on again. Now I was *'told'* to go to Puttaparthi and Sai Baba's Ashram.

I was *'told'* I was to use his facilities. I didn't know what that meant but off we went. The young man God had shown me to take me there was brilliant he knew the railway, bus system and the short cuts from place to place.

We got to Sai Baba's Ashram. I was *'told'* we had to go in separate. I didn't know why and I couldn't tell him not to come with me, so we went in together. They asked for my passport, he was told there was no room for him, it was full but I was *'told'* it was because he was with me.

I was *'told'* I could stay. I told him to wait at the gates for me and I would be back for him. As I was taken to the office they took my details and took my passport.

"Oh Irish," they said, "this is the only Irish passport here!" They asked about my country - Ireland, about the fighting. Then they took the passport and said, "You get it back tomorrow. You have a talk," and told me where to go. Then they said, "You have to get a photo taken and bring it back here, you can get it done outside," they said, "you will be in Hall 'A'."

"Fine," I said.

I was taken across to a huge place packed with people. I'd never been in an ashram before, but it felt ok.

I was worried about my friend at the gate waiting for me. As I got to Hall 'A' there was a lovely woman there taking my name.

This was a huge hall and everyone was sleeping side by side on the floor with lots of mosquito nets and washing hanging around.

I put my bag down at my space. I was going to sleep on the floor but I was *'told'* - *'get a bed'*. I asked the lady, "Where do I get a bed - outside the main gate?"

"A man will show you."

Off I went, thinking (how am I going to carry a bed all this way!) I saw my friend at the gate and told him that I had to get a photo and bed. I went to get the photo done first. I was told, "Brush the hair from your forehead." I did then the man took it.

We waited a few minutes and I got the photo, four small ones.

The man said, "Look!"

I was *'told'* to look. As I did I had a white round mark on my forehead - the third eye. I couldn't believe it and I looked dark, the man with me said he wanted one. Then we asked where we get a bed. Off we went to the shop.

People were queued up for beds, westerners and all nationalities. I saw an Indian man taking one bed back and I was *'told'* I was to have that bed (a sun bed) but not the mattress, so I asked for that bed.

The man checked it to make sure it was ok. Then I had to pay 300 rupees, which you got back when you brought the bed back. The man said he would carry it in for me.

I was *'told'* I was to be here for just three days.

I got the bed set up and off I went to see my friend again to get him somewhere to stay close by for the night. Then I told him next day to come into the Ashram on his own and he would get in and he did.

Men were placed together and women on their own, unless married couples came, they were placed together.

Each time I came in and out the lovely big tree just inside the main gates had a lovely Aura coming from it. There were candles burning by it, like we did at home years ago, bits of cloth and ribbons tied on it. People prayed by it.

This place had phones. You could phone anywhere in the world, post, stamps and use banks to change money. It had two eating-places with food for Indians and Westerners. I wasn't eating much, just bananas and water. But here I was *'told'* to eat the food.

I went in to see what the food was like and it was lovely. The food had an aura, which means it was good food. As I went in the queue for food I got fruit and cake, it tasted lovely.

I phoned my family and went to bed. Next Morning I was out of my body. Again I found myself standing behind my head looking down on myself. I then looked across at the two Indian women talking, sitting looking at me sleeping. Then I woke up, sat up, looked around and no one was here, only me.

"Where is everyone?" I said.

"Gone to see Swami," they said.

I didn't know what that meant. I later learnt they all go three or four in the morning to get a good place to see the holy man - Sai Baba.

Then I set off and saw this huge pile of shoes and crowds of people. I went in but was stopped by a woman because I didn't have anything on my shoulders (a scarf). But my shoulders were covered so I went off. As I walked around I saw a man falling. He hit the back of his head and it was bleeding badly. People gathered around him, the stewards and helpers of the Ashram trying to help.

I was *'told'* – *'take three leaves from the tree and put them on his head, it will stop the bleeding'*. I put my hand on the steward's arm to tell him, he didn't even look up to my face just to my white hand on his arm and he pushed me back. I went to talk to him again and again he pushed me back with his arm, but it was done in an aggressive way. I felt his anger, so I went off.

Then I was told I was to eat, so I went off to get something. We were all queued up. There was porridge. I couldn't believe it.

There were beautiful fruitcakes, breads, pizza and all sorts of food. I can tell if food is ok or not, by the auras colour surrounding it and this food was really good.

There were lots of bowls of porridge and there was one big bowl there. I was *'told'* to take the big one. While I was thinking about it a big lady behind me put her hand over it and took it.

I took another and went on. I loved the food and it cost just a few rupees. Next I was *'told'* - *look around at the people*. Their plates were piled high with food and yet places where I had just been had nothing to eat.

I wonder if these people even thought of that.

Then I saw them outside the Ashram, buying all sorts of things and having dresses and saris made for them in pure silk.

I was *'told'* to listen to one woman being measured. She had an American accent and was speaking to the tailor man sharply, "And what are you going to line it with?" she asked.

I never heard her say 'please' or 'thanks' once.

Looking at some of these Western women, it was like a fashion parade, with their different saris, some acted as if they owned the place.

I spoke to some people who have come to this ashram for over ten years and wouldn't go outside the gates. I asked, "Why not, that's how you learn things - see things, talk to the people."

"Oh there are only robbers and beggars outside," one said.

"Is that all you can see?" I said. She looked at me and I walked away.

Then there was the woman who wanted to shower three or four times a day. I had come from places where they had NO water and some girls had to walk miles to get an urn full every day. Do these women want to know this?

I watched as they filled their bins with wet toilet paper. As they were told not to put it down the toilets, the drains couldn't take it here. I watched, as the bins were so full they put the paper on the ground and then watched a young Indian girl struggled to carry it from the toilets through the hall to a door at the other end and not one lady offered to help her.

I went to help. She was so shocked.

"No! No!" she said.

"Yes! Yes!" I said and we laughed.

Then I heard a woman talking, a few beds from me, to an American woman. I was told to listen. The Polish woman was telling her to go see a girl in another block about a massage.

Then I was *'told'* I had to see this girl. I asked the Polish girl if she would come with me to see her.

"Yes," she said. Next evening we went over to her room, her aura was lovely. She told me to take my clothes off, the top half.

"Oh, I have never done that before in front of people."

She looked at me.

"Do not be afraid," she said, "you are alright here."

I was *'told'* to go along with it. As I started to undress the other women started to leave, so there was just four of us left in the room, this girl was also Polish.

159

She worked on my back and head, talking to my body, as she was working along it. "You are beautiful," she said, "don't carry the weight of the world on your shoulders."

I just cried.

"That's it, let it out," she said as she worked away, "that is all your body will give up at the moment. Will you come back tomorrow for another go?"

As I was leaving I went to pay her. "No, no," she said, "I do not take anything, I am in Sai Baba's holy place and if I can help someone, I will." She would not take anything - we left.

Then I saw the holy man. He looked the same as he looked in the photo a friend had shown me; in the photo he had a halo of black hair. I kept looking at him from a distance I couldn't see an aura, but his body looked different, but I didn't know how.

I woke up next morning as everyone was gone again and the woman was sitting at the bottom of my bed now. I got on very well with them.

I overslept again. Then I went down to the big hall where everyone was. I was told to go to the men's side. I was 'told' they will see me as an Indian man. As I walked slowly up the men's side I couldn't believe it. No one was shouting to me to go to the other side. I was there for over half an hour. I watched Sai Baba go around to the women and men. Then I felt something drop around me. I was told to watch as the men came running towards me.

"Go back! Go back!" They told me and pointed to me to the other side.

Then my Indian friend came in and was in the hall near me on the other side. We were talking one day about everything and an American woman asked why I was talking to him.

"Oh," I said, "we are friends."

"You are friends," she said, "I do not think so."

"Oh," I said, "he works here," trying to get rid of her.

"I do not think so," she said again. "I will call someone about you." Then she said, "Is he working for you?"

I said, "We work together."

160

She was not having any of it. She called a man over. My friend said we were friends. The man said, "How are you *friends?*"

I said, "We have known each other before we came here."

He told us not to speak to each other again, that this was a special place and we should be quiet and prayerful and he went off.

I told my friend I would see him outside the gate on the third day, and thought to myself I am doing God's work, we both are.

Then I was *'told'* to change my money here. I was having a lot of trouble changing my traveller's cheques. At one place I went around to three banks. When we got to the forth one I was sent from one person to the other, then they wanted to photocopy my passport. One of the boys that was with me went out and got it done.

Then they asked if I have changed money before. I said, "Yes."

So they wanted to photocopy the receipt of that. Luckily I had one in my bag. At one point they laughed at my surname.

One woman was worse than the other. Then I got the money.

"You have to wait now for a receipt," she said.

I said, "I can't. I have to catch a train."

Off we went. Despite all our problems all the banks had the change currency sign on their doors.

So now I knew what was meant when I was *'told'* I was to use Sai Baba's facilities. I changed a lot of money here with no problem at all and the food was really good. I also used the shops for food and I bought two saris for friends. But I was told to get another sari and which one to get. It was a beautiful orange. I would be *'told'* in time who it was for.

Then I was *'told'* to send a card to my uncle in Ireland, he was 93 and unwell. So I did that and was *'told'* to walk to my left. As I did there was a man cutting coconuts for a drink. I was *'told'* to drink. As I was drinking I saw a man coming towards me, he had a light purple aura around him. As he got near me I started

161

to talk to him in a different language. I didn't know what I was saying. I thought I talked to him for a few minutes.

The man beside me, now with a smile on his face said, "Ah, you speak German."

(German) I thought, (what did I say to him?) I couldn't ask him so I said, "Oh no, I don't speak much."

"Ah," he said, "just a little, it was good."

We carried on talking; he was here with his partner. This was the first time for him to be here, as he was into a different religion, but his partner asked him to come and just see Sai Baba for himself. But because they were not married, she was in one part with the women and he was on the men's side. He said he liked what he saw and heard and was glad he had come.

He said he was getting married later in the year. So when they come again they will be together. Then he said, "I have a fear of galvanise? Where I am staying now I have fear," he smiled, and said, "from years ago I think."

With that I *saw* him in the past (sitting shaking and sweat running off him in a war bunker) then I was *'told'* to tell him to take two bottles of rescue remedy$_2$.

But I couldn't tell him, what would he think?

He told me he was so stuck in his own religion that he would not look at anyone else's religion, only his own. I said, "I was the same once." We said goodbye and off we went.

Then the last day I felt fit, healthy and really good. But I sensed I hadn't put anything back into the ashram. I thought I would leave a donation, but straight away I was *'told'* – *'No, my money was to go elsewhere'.*

I was *'told'* to go and see the lady that worked on my back and leave 500 rupees in an envelope. So I put the money in an envelope and put her name on it. I was *'told'* - *go now.*

As I set off the lights in the ground led me the way to go. Then just in front of me was the German I had talked to the day before, the chance of seeing him, again with thousands of people here.

I was *'told'* tell him. As we said hello to each other I said I would be leaving later, and then I told him.

162

I said, "I don't know what you will make of this but God *'told'* me you need two bottles of rescue remedy and take it directly on your tongue." I wrote it all out for him and he said, "Thank you I do have a lot of fear and I will get this when I go back to Germany."

We said goodbye and off I went. I was glad I told him, no matter what he thought of me.

I set off to find the girl but she wasn't there and I couldn't put the envelope under the door and so I went off. I was to go up one road and back another, as I did this I thought 'I have never been down this road before'. I walked on and saw a group of Indian women sitting on the ground. As I got to them made room for me to sit down and watch the holy man, who was walking around. He was leaving the big hall and walking to his house. I asked, "Does he live there?"

"Yes," they said. I was told to stand up, as I did I saw him quite clearly. He was walking towards his front door. But about 5-6 feet before he got to his door I saw the whole figure of him leave his body. It was all light green energy. But I saw his eyes in this energy. I said, "Hello," to the energy."

"You can *see* me?"

"Yes, I can *see* you."

I watched as Sai Baba looked around and then went inside. So I couldn't see his aura, but I knew something was different about his body, and this was it – "Spiritual Energy". When this energy is with you, you can see, hear and KNOW.

I went off to get my bag. I left the envelope on my Polish friend's pillow and asked the girl opposite to tell her to give it to her Polish friend, the girl who did the massage.

I set off, as I was walking out with the Indian man carrying my bed I saw the man who took my passport photo in. I asked if I could see Sai Baba for a minute. I told him I'm writing a book and this place will be in it.

"Oh good," he said, "when you finish your book bring it here and Swami will sign it and bless it for you," (with that I *heard - it is already blessed*).

I said, "Goodbye," and said, "I'll be back," and we laughed.

"Give my regards to Ireland!" he shouted.

"I will," I said, as I was walking out I felt uplifted and glad I had listened to come here.

But we do need to talk to people at times. Look what happened in just a few days.

Then as I got to the gate I was *'told'* - *'give the man your bed'*. (What!) I thought, again, - *'give the man your bed'*. (Some men work in the ashram carrying beds and bags for a few rupees or whatever they are given).

I looked at the man. I said, "Do you want this bed?"

I was surprised when he said, "Yes please!" bowing his head. So how do I go about doing this, I thought? I went over to the shop and said, "I will buy the bed but give me a receipt for this for the man to keep or the bed will be taken off him." I was also *'told'* to give him money and I did this.

Then a white woman came over and said, "Hello!" She told me she is working here teaching the young children and helping them to go to school. She told me she buys things here and takes them to her own country to sell and this helps the people. She told me the man I gave the bed to has two children, they all sleep on the floor and he has kidney problems. At least now he will be off the floor. "Very, very poor," she said.

As I was on the bus I saw a huge poster (very old) of George Best (the footballer) that made me smile.

Then I saw a huge poster of president Clinton of America with the words, *'Is Bill Clinton really innocent? Find out in next week's papers,'* this also brought a smile to my face.

While in a rickshaw coming from a village I was changing from a sari back to my trousers. I had just started taking the sari off, there were big lorries coming towards us on the opposite side. With that the driver pulls right across the road in front of this lorry. My head went one way, my legs the other, as it stopped he jumped out and walked off. I thought what's wrong? I finished dressing and went to him. He was smoking, sweating and shaking.

"What's wrong?" I asked.

He couldn't talk. He was in panic, "What's up?" He couldn't get it out and pointed to me changing. I was wearing my trousers under my sari and I left the little sari top on and just put a tee shirt over it. So I wasn't uncovered in anyway but it shocked him.

I said, "I'm sorry, I didn't think." As I looked back my sari was hanging out the seat of the rickshaw. We had stopped at a petrol station and eating-place. As I talked to him I was *'told'* to look at the boy beyond him, in the back. As I did he was staring at me, he was well dressed and groomed. I was *'told'* - *'keep watching'* this boy couldn't take his eyes off me (because I am white - I suspect) he never looked where he was going. Just kept looking at me, then I watched as he walked right into a fresh cowpat, a big one. Oh his foot was full of it! I looked away quickly; as he looked around to me I didn't want him to see I had seen it. I couldn't stop laughing. Then I thought it's the first time I have laughed in years. I was told to take him in for a drink. In we went. A young boy came out. His aura was shining. I was *'told'* to give him money. He had a limp, as one leg was shorter than the other. As we left I gave him the money but he wouldn't take it. I asked the owner if he could take the money for him. "Yes," he said and I told him it was to help him. He looked and smiled, "Thank you."

The driver had calmed down. He was a lovely fella. I was always *'told'* which driver to go with and they all stayed with me and helped me and really looked after me and carried my bags.

I remember one took me to his church and as we walked up this steep hill he was sweating and saying, "I am a Catholic, I am a Catholic, I am a Catholic." It made me laugh.

The priest's house was at the bottom of the hill and the priest had his leather shoes on and good clothes. He did not do the hill walk very often.

I spoke to a young boy who had his tongue burnt as a punishment because he was not learning. The dad beat him, his brother and mother. They were told not to talk to uneducated people; the father had treated them like this.

I said, "It is time to stop. A time to speak up…"

In Calcutta I spoke up to the priests and nuns. I told them what was happening all over India. The land being taken from the people, the physical and sexual abuse, that's all I was told to say for now, then I was *'told'* - *'be careful what you say, it will be carried'.*

I was out with a friend and while on the bus I felt as if something had ripped my side. I felt I wanted to move. There were two women beside me, one with a baby on her lap. They were talking to two men in front of them. Standing up I was *'told'* - *'Move your bag! Pull it in front of you!'* I did and then I got off the bus. As I went to buy something I noticed my bag had been ripped down the side with a knife. It must have been the women beside me with the baby on her lap. If I hadn't moved my bag my money and passport would have been taken. When I asked someone what happened to me I was told, "Oh they do that, get on buses to rob people." So I thought, (oh that's that then) and I thought no more of it.

Then another day, as we were getting off the bus I noticed two men dressed very well, they were not poor, wearing leather shoes, cashmere jumpers and good trousers. They caught me between their shoulders, pressing into me. I had carrier bags and they had little silver hooks that were tearing into my bags. One said to keep my mouth shut or it will happen to me.

They pulled away. It was all over in a few seconds. I showed my friend the bag and all the holes in it. I said, "Why did they do this?"

"I don't know," she said.

But it worried us; we kept looking behind to make sure they were not following us.

I said, "We will get a rickshaw back." I was told to say nothing about this.

An old lady said to me, "I am so worried for you. You must be very, very careful." She was frightened herself. I wondered what she had heard.

Then I thought I would stay in for a few days. As I sat I was *'told'* to look up to the roof opposite. As I did I saw a man looking at me, he had something in his hand and he knew I had

166

seen him, he put the object to his mouth and said, "She has seen me." It was like I was standing beside him. He was using a mobile phone and I have never, in all the places I had been to in India, seen anyone with a mobile phone.

Now I was worried. What is going on? I was told before, people had their passports taken off them and told not to come back again. All their details were taken and then if they wanted to come again they would not be able to come again, they would not get a visa.

I had two weeks to go. I couldn't go out, I was afraid to go out. Then I saw the vision again, of me at home and the clothes I was in. So I thought I'm going to be ok. God will look after me. After a few days I was *'told'* to go and change my dates to come back I was given the date, so I got a taxi with a friend and set off to the travel shop. But I was told there are no seats, all are booked up and was informed they would phone me if they get a seat.

Two days passed and off I went to them again. "No," they told us, "nothing," as we were getting ready to leave the machine started to go. I was *'told'* - *'this is your seat'*.

The woman said, "You are very lucky a seat is cancelled and it is the 27th day. The day I was *'told'* I would be leaving.

So I set off next day to buy a few things, feeling better, but I stayed away from people, as I didn't want to get anyone in trouble.

Then my friend and I were asked to a meal. As we walked and were waiting to cross the street I was *'told'* – *'take your friend and move to the left - NOW!'* As I did this we heard something fall to the ground. It was a woodcutter, had a wooden round handle, about 18 inches long, with sharp edges all around its front and sides. It was new.

Then I heard a man's voice, "That was just a warning, if it was meant, it would have hit you."

But it would have hit my back if I hadn't been told to move to my left! I was told by the same voice – "Do not look around, if it was meant to hit you it would have."

We got to Mary's friends they came back with us, but there was no sign of anything.

I was given a meal, then I started to cough, I couldn't stop. Then I was shown the cook putting brown stuff, from a bottle all over my meal. I asked my friend if she shook something on my meal.

"Yes," she said.

"Did she put it on yours?" I asked.

"No," she said.

Then I was asked are you a reporter?

"No," I said and laughed. "I'm here because God wanted me to see what was going on. Nothing more was said. I was *'told'* later that the brown stuff on my food was rat poison.

I was so ill the nun wanted me to go to a sanatorium.

"No," I said, "I'll be going home soon. I'll be ok."

The nuns looked after me - they were so good. Some would come and talk, bringing me drinks.

Then one evening I was reading on the bed and I saw a huge vision of Sister M. She was kneeling by the bed, bringing her arms up and down on the bed. The arms went right down through me. She was crying and in so much pain. She had cancer (the church says bear it well, it's suffering for God. But it's not. I was *'told'* while looking at her *'She is as innocent today as she was when she left Ireland'.*

Next I was taken to a graveyard and shown grave stones of Irish girls that went into the convent in Ireland and were sent to India. I was told a lot died on the long boat journey over and a lot died with the heat and conditions here in India.

I couldn't help thinking, 'If only the Mammies of these girls knew this. Yet, still to this day the Church is taking girls from homes and sending them somewhere else. They can't even keep their birthdays that they were born with. They take a saint's name and have that feast day as their birthday. Again, I was *'told'* — *'It is all wrong'.*

I saw nun's open letters read them and if any money was in the letters put it in their pockets

168

One orphan woman told me one nun was really good. When she finished school the nun gave her money from her sponsor to give to her gran. Some people felt the nuns did help them learn to cook, clean, sew and type. But they don't like what is going on with the widespread abuse and that is why now it has to be stopped. The whole thing needs to be looked into.

The evening before I left India in '98 I was really worried. I was to come home in the year of Jan '99, but *'told'* to change the date.

Then this beautiful white light came into the room. It was two whites; the clear white was inside the misty white like smoke and I heard "whom to fear" I was *'told'* to open the bible. As I did there it was - the page. I couldn't believe it. I was *'told'* to read₃.

A nun gave this bible to me a few weeks before I was going to give it away, but I was *'told'* to keep it (I gave away the rosaries though).

Notes

The picture at the front of the chapter is of the symbol OM.

    1.   'May' was a lady that worked with Mother Teresa when she was first starting out with her charitable work.

    2.   'Rescue Remedy' is a homeopathic medicine for use against panic attacks and similar symptoms of fear.

    3.

Luke 12

Matt 10.28-31   Whom to fear

Luke 11

Matt 10: 26-27 A warning against Hypocrisy

Chapter 15

Back in England and Work Again

While shopping in a superstore with my grandson I went into a café to get a drink and chips for him. As he was finished I was *'told'* to ask for a job. I was really surprised but asked the girl, who was picking up the trays, "Are there any jobs here?"

She told me to go to the service counter and ask. She thought there were jobs available. As I was making my way to the counter I was *'told'* I would get a job upstairs and Molly would be of help to me.

I thought, (There is no upstairs, here it is all on the flat and I will ask for a job filling shelves). I got the form, filled it out and handed it back. A couple of days later I had a phone call to go for an interview. There was a group of us there - men and women.

When the interview was over we were told there were jobs for porters and a job in the staff canteen, as one lady was off sick and 'Molly' could do with help.

When I heard the name 'Molly' the hairs on my arms came up. She asked me, "Would you be interested in catering?"

I wasn't sure about that. I hadn't done it before then I was *'told' – 'take it.'* I reluctantly said, "Yes."

"Good!" she said, "it's in the staff canteen 'upstairs'." It was just as I had been told.

On my first day I was very nervous but all went well. When I saw Molly for the first time I could not help thinking (what was going to unfold in this job?)

I was only there three days and we had to go to a meeting all about the shop, how far it had come and where it was going into the future year 2000. There was a women talking, then a man came in with some papers

I was sitting at the back. The talk finished I was *'told'* – *'Ask about the poor countries'* (from where most of the things were coming from). The room was full and I could not do it. Then I went back to my job in the canteen. A little while later the women from the talk came in and I was *'told'* – *'talk to her now'*.

I felt terrible. I had only been there for three days! Then I was in front of her. My heart pounding I said, "What are you doing about the poor countries. Doing something for the poor countries would be good for the future. It would be good going into the year 2000."

Well the look I got could have knocked me down. "We have our team that looks after that!" she said.

I was going to say more but she walked away.

I later found out that they send the old stores staff's dresses and trousers to the poor countries when they change them. 'Oh,' I thought, 'that will really help them!' The poor do not want our cast offs, why should they have that. Nylon clings to you in India under the intense heat. Some only had one sari washed and put it back on.

A few weeks went by and one day the manager came in, to my surprise. Molly told him what I did and would he help. He asked to see the photos. Then I was told to tell him what is going on. As I was leaving one day he was coming up the stairs. I was *'told'* to tell him but I could not. I clocked out and was leaving when he came out of one of the offices. I was told to tell him now. I did.

I told him what I was *'told'* to tell him. The next day I took in some things for him to see, newspaper clippings and things. So he could see I was telling the truth, he looked shocked. But that was it I never heard anymore.

It was now June. I was *'told'* I was to go to Ireland. My mam needed help. I was *'told'* what week to go and to my surprise no one was on holiday that week. As I arrived in the house my mam looked very tired. She also wanted to talk to me and visit a few places. It worked out well as my sister was away and I could use her car she said.

While out walking one day I noticed a light by an estate agents window. I walked towards it. Then it moved to a card in the window which had *'For Sale - An old cottage with galvanised tin roof'* written on it. I went and asked details. I was *'told'* to go see it, as I got to the gate my brother said, "It's got a lovely feel to it".

Then I was *'told'* to watch the door, as I did it opened. There was no one by the door. I shouted to my brother to look at the door again. It was shut. I could not understand it, but the feeling of as if I had been here before was overwhelming. But I had not. I went back to the agent, I was told to offer no more than £23,000, it had no toilet or water but I was not worried about that. But the price kept rising by £500 a time. I even went to see the owners, after I found out who they were.

At the old cottage in the garden to the left of me I saw a round light so bright. Then the scene got bigger and I saw three tents, like Indian ones, it looked like animal skin around the tents. Then my eyes went to the bottom of the tents. It was about 5cm's from the ground. I saw animal bone holding it together; it was about 1m wide and flat. There was a fire and it felt so warm. Then I was *'told'* the stone I got from new grange (a year earlier) was to be put back here. I have not been told when yet.

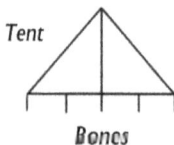

Tent

Bones

When I met the daughter of the house she had the most beautiful aura. It was like patchwork colours all around her, wide and high. I was *'told'* to shake her hand. But I did not, as I had not shook the other people's hands.

I put a bid in for £20,000 then £23,000. Then my mam and sister wanted to see it. So I took them out in my brother's car. As we walked around it I was *'told'* to put my arms around my mam. (I did not know how I was going to do this. I had never done it before). With that, my mam, who was walking down the garden beside my sister and me said laughing, "I'll give you a few pounds towards it."

Then I put my left hand on her left arm and my right hand around her back and on her right arm. Laughing I squeezed her and shouted to my sister, laughing, "Did you hear that Julia! Mammy is going to lend me a few pounds. Do you have a few pounds too? Have a share of it." We all laughed. But I knew she had a lot of healing. She also knew something had happened as I had squeezed her, as she had felt so innocent and nice.

Then I was *'told'* the next day I had to walk on the beach and sit on the rocks.

I saw this huge swerve of energy coming towards me. I was *'told'* – *'look around; they have destroyed the beach by placing huge rocks to stop the tide. Later you will not see the stones for the sand and it will not stop the tide. They have done MORE damage'*.

Then I was in Cornwall again and back at work. I saw a lot of staff at work whose auras were not very good. A lot were eating far too much - they were making themselves bad. Then I found out the food we eat is frozen for up to twenty years! A lot of the time I could see the food was not good and had a dreadful smell at times. But the work in the cafe certainly helped me cope with what I had seen in India.

I was also *'told'* to undercharge some people and over charge other times, only one person told me I undercharged her but all told me I overcharged them. With some people I knew they were going to be sick. Then some would complain for no reason at all, the food was this or that.

People do not like to queue in these supermarket stores for long. So when this happens staff are taken from their own jobs to go on the tills[1].

Before I went to Ireland, there was a price war on between two vegetable shops. Potatoes etc. selling for 5p to 10p a pound, bananas selling sometimes for as little as 10p a pound and I saw little children beaten for taking a banana because they were hungry. These bananas had to be packed for western countries that have it all and still play their silly games.

The price war between the two vegetable shops in my home town went on for weeks, it made radio, and TV and I watched people queuing for one and half-hours with baskets. I saw them walking on the fruit falling from their overflowing baskets and no one complaining because they were getting something for next to nothing. Their purses were full of money.

One of these shops closed and then later so did the other shut down.

In India by comparison people were in rubbish dumps looking for scraps to eat. Men, women and children with animals!

When I just got back from India for the third time I was devastated. Everything I had grown up with, which I thought was truth and good was actually very bad. So my foundations were rocked.

Then I saw a huge, white light, with a glow. I was shown myself as I first went to India in the August of 1994. I looked in good health with a good aura around me. As it faded, up came another. I was told that was you with the lies. This is you with the truth: I could see my head was in a state; my body was like a dress all ripped and had big red spots all over it. It was like I had been put into a cage with lions and they had ripped me to pieces. As it faded I then saw myself in a big field of lovely long, green grass with red poppies all over.

I was *'told'* - *'now you have to heal, the people will be there to help you and you will be told what to take and what to do to help yourself'*.

174

As that faded up came a beautiful rose, pink colour. I could see someone in the distance, as it got clearer I could see my mam. She looked so young, the same as the photos I had seen of her. She was laughing and looking very happy. I could feel her happiness - it felt as if I could touch her joy. Then she turned to face me. I was shown all around her stomach was a beautiful light red colour of misty light. As the mist faded I could see a baby in her stomach. I knew the baby was me before I was told, I was lying sideways. I was *'told'* this was your choice, your task.

At that the picture faded. I saw a huge figure. It was a deep purple colour. As he came towards me he had a gigantic brown covered book, really old. I thought it would be too heavy for me to carry (thinking he was going to place it in my arms).

As he stood in front of me the energy bent over and as he put the book at my feet I thought, (Oh, this is going to be too heavy and hurt). But as he put it down over my feet it was as light as a feather. I was *'told'* – *'look down'*. As I did I read on the cover and also *'heard'* - ***"The Book of Knowledge, use it wisely"***.

Notes

The picture at the front of the chapter is of the English flag.

    1.   When shop staff are used in this way they are called 'queue busters'.

Chapter 16
Home Again in Ireland

A few months later I was *'told'* to go to Ireland again on the 28th July for one month. My contract of employment was still valid but I said I would leave. I knew I had to go again for a reason. I was going to live like a hermit for a month. I wanted and needed some peace.

My friend and I went to buy a tent, but when we were looking at them in the stones I was *'told'* - *'No tent!'*

So I left it and went by train and ferry to Ireland. Again I was *'told'* to go to 'Clair' and to go with the flow.

On the ferry I was *'told'* to go also to Achill. I had heard of this name before but I couldn't think where it was. It was a lovely sailing trip. I was on deck and really feeling great. I took very little clothes but I did take my trousers and boots. What a journey this turned out to be. My sister had said she would like to go to Clair and she would drive. I was going to travel on this journey by myself but I was told to go with her. However, for a couple of days she had things to do, and then at the weekend we would set off.

One day she had to go to 'Carlow Stores'. I was 'told' to go. I had never been there even though I had been out with a man who had lived there. He used to be in the army and would walk or cycle to my home. I could not believe it was so far away.

I liked the town. As we were going back out of Carlow I saw a sign for the Dolmen. I was 'told' to go and see it. My sister, not a bit interested in these stores drove on, then she said, "Did you want to see it?"

"Yes," I said.

She turned back and waited in the car. As I made my way through the path in the field it was a damp day with surrounding white mist. As I walked further in I remembered it was Thursday 1 July 1999. This was a very beautiful burial place all marked out with sheep fencing in the fields around it.

As I turned right into the path of the stones there was a black sheep, just in front of me. I looked around and wondered where it had come from. The sheep looked at me and started moving in front of me. Just then I 'heard' - 'The black sheep has returned'. I looked around me, no one was there but me. As I walked to the stones I was 'told' - 'Walk around the stones from left to right, anti-clockwise then go inside underneath big stone and sit to the four winds'.

As I sat on the stone looking to the front of me for a while, I felt a pull within my stomach, as I turned to my left I sat for a moment then around again, my head slightly bent. Then I turned around again and back to the front. I sat for a moment then all of a sudden I felt a quick, sudden pull in my right side. It was so quick it did not hurt. I felt as if I had to pass urine. I had a job to hold on. I knew something had happened, but I did not know what. It was as if my breath had been taken away as I sat for a few minutes it passed and I was ok.

It was now time to leave, as I walked away I said, "Thank you." As I walked back down the field to the car some people were coming up the hill, they were foreign. I told them to sit inside the stone. I felt wonderful! - I had so much energy. This started on my way to the stones. I got lighter and lighter. I felt

177

great, I did not understand what had happened or what it meant but it felt wonderful and good. As I got near the car I thought (this is only the first day of the month and see what has happened already).

Then we set off to the West of Ireland, stopping as we went to look at towns and eat.

We were right on time for the last ferry crossing the River Shannon, just after 9pm. We drove on to the ferry and sailed across. It was lovely and calm with a beautiful sunset in the sky. It looked lovely. I felt a great presence halfway across the Shannon I was *told'* – *'get out of the car'*. As we got out my sister walked around. I stood by the car and edge of the ferry. Then I was *'told'* - *'stand to the four winds'*. I looked at the other cars, some drivers were out looking around, some sitting in their cars.

I was *'told'* not to take any notice of them and to do it again. My body stretched up and I went around just stopping for a couple of seconds, the same as Carlo, but standing on the ferry in the middle of the River Shannon. It was then that I got back into the car. I felt so refreshed and surprised as we drove off the ferry and made our way left to Kilrush.

We thought we better get a bed and breakfast place, as it was now getting late and my sister had driven a long way. Then I saw a sign saying 'Katie O'Conner Hostel'. I was *'told'* we had to stay there as we drove on I said, "We will stay at a hostel."

My sister was not very keen on this, but went along with it.

As we got to Kilrush I went and knocked on the door. Then I heard a man's voice call out from the shop alongside. "Come in, come in," he said with a lovely smile.

A woman was shopping. The till was wide open with all the money in it. I said, "I am looking for a place to stay." With that a woman came forward from the back.

I said, "Do you run next door?"

"Yes," she said. She had a wonderful aura, the whole place did. I told her it was for myself and sister.

"The place is full. A man who stays there often had just rang to book his room with his daughter, the last one."

178

I liked this - she was honest and would not give his room away

I asked, "Have you got anywhere we could sleep? It was just for the night and it is getting dark."

As I was told to stay there I just stood looking at her. She was the homely sort. She felt sorry for us.

"Well, I only have the store room."

"That's fine," I said.

She looked at me, "I will show you first."

I got my sister and she took us through a long hallway full of bikes. The front door was code locked for safety. She took us into a big kitchen where she had a big fire lit. It felt warm and lovely.

"You can eat here or outside it's up to you," she said as we went upstairs and into the storeroom. It was lovely and clean and there were five pine single beds in it and a bathroom just beside it.

"This will be fine," I said, not looking at my sister.

"But we haven't any sheets, I will give you sheets."

They were lovely and warm.

Then we went out to look around. I felt I had been here before. The wide streets, the houses three stories high, clean and painted lovely colours.

As we walked down the main street and at the bottom overlooking a river I remembered this was the vision I saw with me running up behind my husband of now, but in a different time. He was dressed in a brown jacket with trousers coming just below his knees, long cream stockings and brown shoes. We were in our late 20's age wise. I was shouting his name, but as I went to put my hand on his shoulder the vision stopped. I had been with him in another life. I felt as if I wanted to live there.

We walked back to the pub, had a drink and went back to the hostel.

Next morning we went and had breakfast in the café across the street. It was very good. We walked around again. Got some scones in the shop where they are baked on the premises.

We went and got our bags, said goodbye and set off to our next destination.

As we drove on we got to Spanish Point. At Spanish Point we walked along the beach. As we were coming away I saw a vision of a little child I knew and also saw a man I had never seen before. I was *'told'* to get her a red knit bracelet. I saw the whole thing come in front of me. As we went to Miltown I got one for her (the girl's father was dead).

In Miltown Malbay we stopped. Here we came across a set dancing school. As my sister liked this and goes to set dancing we went into the hall. The music was great and we both had a few dances. One man showed me the steps. I enjoyed it but I am no dancer! Then we were told there was a big dance that evening, so we decided to stay and have a bed and breakfast and go on the next day. As we looked for a place to stay the town was packed. There was a lot going on, street entertainment girls putting coloured ribbons in hairs. I was *'told'* to have my hair done; I even had the colours picked for me, to my sister's surprise.

She said, "Are you having it done?"

"Yes," I said.

I queued with the young girls. As I got down on my knees to have a strand of my hair done a white band of light came around the colours I had to have in my hair. The girl that did my hair had an aura around her. As I picked the colours my sister said the blue would look better on you. I said, "I like this." My hair was short so it did not take long. Then on the way around town we came across The Will Clancy School of Music and the people learning the set dancing. There were people here from all around the world. They had come to learn Irish music and dance. There was so much going on and I never knew anything like this was going on in Ireland. It was so lovely to see parts of Ireland I had not seen before. I had a great feeling of excitement inside.

As we went around the streets asking for bed and breakfast we found everyone full. So then I saw a card in a shop restaurant window offering bed and breakfast. We went in to ask, but again we were told it had gone, all were full.

As we started to leave I saw a light go around some people sitting having tea, the light went around two people in particular. As we got outside a woman came up behind me as we were walking away. She tapped me on the shoulder and said I have a bed, you can stay with me, we both looked at each other and my sister asked her some questions. I saw the light around her and knew it would be fine The lady told us she had just come back to Ireland to live and had bought a bungalow here. She told us where to find it and she would be home with us in two hours. She could not remember the name of the bungalow. My sister looked at me funny, wondering if this would be ok or not. But looking at these two women with the light going around them they looked like sisters.

Anyway we parted saying we would see them in a couple of hours. My sister was not really sure. We went in some pubs, the music or 'crack' as they say in Ireland, was great. There were also children, in the pubs that were very smoky. As I looked at one little child in his mam's arms I could 'see' his eyes were looking very red. I was *'told'* to keep watching, as the child got sleepy, just before his eyes closed a white mist, in the shape of the child, came up from his body and went right through the ceiling of the pub. I was *'told'* this is how he could cope with it at his age. He was about two years old and still sleeping as we left.

We set off to find the bungalow. As we went down the road I was told to look to my right, as I did I saw the lady at the window.

My sister said, "Are you sure this is it?"

"Yes, I think so." As we drove in there was no one at the window. As we knocked on the door she opened it.

"Oh," she said, with a big smile to us. "I must apologise for coming after you today earlier. I do not know what came over me. I have never done that before. What must you think of me?" We all laughed (I knew it was meant to be).

We had a comfortable place to stay.

I was *'told'* to tell her to take 'Rescue Remedy'.

We talked and got on so well that we promised to call that way again when we were in the area (and I will too).

That evening we set off for the dance. My sister loves dancing. I cannot do it though; I get all embarrassed when I get up. My sister met some friends there. I was asked twice to get up and dance. I could not believe it I saw the first man I had seen in a vision a few days earlier. I was saying to him as he asked me up, "I couldn't do it!" Then I was *told* to get up and I enjoyed it. As I sat down I was *'told'* you could still enjoy yourself and do what you are doing. It is what is inside you that counts.

We stayed a while, my sister showing me a few dances and we enjoyed it. Next day we set off early, giving a lift to the little girl helping in the bungalow. I was *'told'* to tell her to have coloured strings put in her hair as I had. She said she wanted to have them done that day. She had a lovely aura around her. We let her off and set out for the cliffs of Moher.

We stopped at Lahinch, walked around the shops and had something to eat. Then we set off again with my sister driving. When we got to the cliffs it was misty but light. The place was packed with visitors. As we walked to the cliff's edge I saw a man lying face down, looking over the cliffs on his belly. I was *'told'* I was to do the same. (I don't know) I thought. As we jumped over the wall to walk to the cliffs edge we had a photo taken of us. We asked a lad sitting on the wall to take it. He was American. As we got down to the cliff's edge I just lay down on my belly and looked over the edge and all around looking at the lovely birds coming in and flying out. There were fulmars, shags, puffins, guillemots, kittiwakes, razorbills and gulls.

I was *'told'* - *'Look! You have no fear'*, and I hadn't. I could never have done this before. My sister could not do it. The cliffs have a sheer drop of 700ft and the scenery is beautiful. I just wanted to lie there on the ground. It felt as if someone very, very tall was standing over me, I could feel the warmth.

My sister felt afraid for me, she said, "Come on, we'll walk up the other side." We went to the left and I saw a circle of men and women lying on the ground holding hands. I was *'told'* – *'there is no need for this'*. We walked on further up the steps to the right. Out in the water I could see something jumping, I was *'told'* – *'It is a dolphin'*. Then I heard people shouting, "Look

182

there's a dolphin out there!" as they got their binoculars out to look. There was great excitement.

As we walked to the top there was a man playing a harp, accompanied by a girl, who was also singing. It was lovely.

We walked past O'Brien's Tower and to the far end I was *'told'* - *'Look to the four winds'*. As I did this clockwise looking at the scenery I said thank you and I thought what an experience. We went into O'Brien's Tower and bought some chocolate for mam.

As we made our way down we went into the café, shops and tourist information office for directions to the Dolmin at Poulnabrone. We wanted to see it and get home to Co Wicklow that evening. They said we would not be able to do it in time.

When making our way back to the car we turned left to make our way around to the Burren, but we realized we could not do it in the daylight remaining and get home. So we drove around until we got to Lisdoonvarna (this is a matchmaking town). People come from all over to find a partner at a certain time of the year. When driving through we nearly reached the stones (having a few miles to go) but it was getting late and so we decided to head on home or we would have to have another bed and breakfast again.

We travelled on a few more miles and suddenly I felt something behind me. It was very hot and I felt it on my head and neck. It was a beautiful feeling. As my sister talked I could not turn to look at her. I could hardly speak; it was like a tight band around my neck. I felt so hot and peaceful. Then my back got very hot. It was like someone lying on my head and back. I still could not move. I tried to look at my sister sideways. It lasted over a few hours then I felt it leave, the smell was of flowers. I was told I got what I needed from the Dolmin Stones and I would be back. The colours were lovely as we drove through three counties in one day and got home at 11pm.

As I walked into the house my mam said you look lovely, you are glowing. I knew she could see the aura. My sister also felt this, but she did not know what was happening. She also felt so peaceful and the lovely smell stayed with us. Everyone in the house asked, "What's that lovely smell." Even my brother smelt it. My sister went off for a drink in the pub. She needed it, she had driven 490miles and we had had no problems.

It had been a very spiritual journey to Co Clair and west of Ireland from the 1st to the 6th July 1999.

Notes

The photograph at the front of the chapter is of Clair.

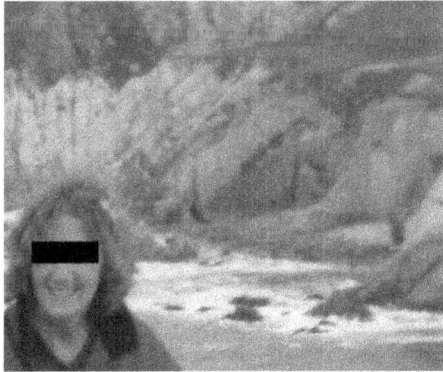

Chapter 17
Achill – Island

Well here I am on the coach on my way to Achill Island. I just can't believe how it has all worked out. I was *'told'* on the ferry to go to Clair and Achill.

I was only in the house a few hours when my mam said, "We are going to Achill Island in a couple of weeks for a few days would you like to come along?"

I just looked at her. "Achill? Yes!" I said. "I would love to go."

She was surprised at my quick reaction as I never go anywhere on coach trips. She said I could see if there were any seats left. She told me the name of the man who was arranging the trip. Next day I couldn't wait to see the man to see if he had a seat (I knew there would be) but I still had to ask and sure enough there was a seat. We were picked up on the 15th July before 6am. I was up at 5am as I couldn't wait to get going. I felt so excited.

We stopped at different places to pick up people and also stopped for dinner, then on to 'Knock'. I was hoping to see a friend at Knock (an old school friend) she lives there. I wasn't going to be taking part in any of the masses or Stations of the

185

Cross, nor did I take part in any of the prayers said on the coach journey. I pray my own way.

I found Knock to be a sham - a rip off! - Especially in the shops and cafes. The Catholic Church is really coining the money in with people paying to have masses and queues of people going to fill their bottles up with 'so-called' holy water.

With that I was shown a vision of the people in India dying for a drink of water and the many that have no water or have to travel miles to get some. Yet, here and other places like this, people are wasting water.

I was *'told'* – *'this water is no different than tap water'*. Some of the people had four or five big plastic containers to fill up and take to their hometown. I wanted to scream, to shout to them, 'for God's sake, wake up! See what you are doing'. But I was *'told'* – *'they don't want to know, they are just living in their own little circle'*.

But it is not living, it is just surviving, their eyes and ears closed shut. They don't want to see or hear what is really going on with some of these 'so called men of God'.

I went on my way, looking around at people going into mass, saying the Stations of the Cross and then going to shops in the street to where a lot of the things were made by the poor in India. I was glad to leave 'Knock'; it had a very cold feeling. The place was all right but what the Catholic Church is doing to it is not.

All places are great it's what people often do to them that is not.

I must say with all the people there that day I only saw one man with the light colours around him and a different colour around his head and ears.

I was *'told'* he is now going to have his eyes and ears opened to the truths.

We got back on the coach. Next stop Achill. Because I booked late I couldn't go with my mam and sister to their bed and breakfast (I knew this). I was put with other people, one woman and two men in a lovely cottage, down by the river looking across to another Island. We were told there was just one family left living there. The view was just breath-taking! Just up the road from us was the 'House of Prayer'. I couldn't be any closer. I was *'told'* this is what I had to 'see'.

On Friday morning 16 July 1999 I walked to the House of Prayer. The place was packed with people sitting outside on chairs and standing everywhere.

I was *'told'* to walk right in. As I went inside there were people sitting in the porches and up the hall. Then I saw a light by the door. I was *'told'* to stand there. I was right under a TV showing the inside of the chapel. As I watched lots of presents, envelopes, flowers and candles arrived at the door. Helpers with arms full brought them in. Then I saw a young girl of about eighteen. She had a lovely aura around her. She stood in front of me and asked if she could help. One of the aids took her outside telling her what he wanted her to do. There was a nun inside the chapel saying the rosary and prayers. I was told this is all they can say. Here mass had been stopped and the Blessed Sacrament taken away. There was a row going on between the priest (Church) and the House of Prayer. Some of the local people told me a lot of it was over money. More people were going to the House of Prayer and not to the Church.

I also saw a lot of buildings going up and a new hotel and new homes being built.

So prayers were said at the House of Prayer and then people could go to the church just down the road for mass. I noticed one or two collections, so the priest was getting his fair share. They had come to an understanding between the Church and the House of Prayer.

They had to because of the new buildings being built. This was going to be big business for them. Just like Lourdes and other places like this.

Then I *'heard'* a voice saying *'here she is'*, as I looked I saw a women standing beside me with another girl trying to get into her room. The door wouldn't open. I looked at Christine and said, "Hello."

"Hello," she said back, with a smile on her face. Then the door opened and she went inside. After a little while she came out again. I put my hand on her arm and said, "Can I talk with you for just a little while please?"

She said, "I can't, but I will pray for your intentions."

I said, "No, no don't do that." She looked at the priest behind her. He pushed her to move and she did and went into the chapel. I was *'told'* – *'it was a nun's convent at one time'*. It had been all done up, including a new roof.

The rosary was being said again. As I looked around the hall and I saw a picture of Mother Teresa it took me back to memories of myself in India in her convent in Calcutta.

Then Christine was passing by me again to get in through the door. She could not get in as there was a security lock on the door. So she and her friend knocked and knocked. They were laughing and talking. Prayers were still being said in the building.

Then the priest came and pressed some numbers but the door still wouldn't open. He pressed three twice then nine twice and still it would not open. I was being *'told'* not to move, I was to stay where I was. Then the door opened from the inside. As it did I saw the place was well furnished, a table was laid with good china and glasses with gold rims all set for dinner (lunch).

After a little while the priest came out again and shouted to the people outside and inside, "If you want medals, pictures, statues or rosaries blessed later go and buy them from the shop." The priest did this three times and people got up and went off. I wondered where the shop was. People put things on their seats so no one could take them while they were gone.

With that a steward came from the room and went to the door of the chapel and shouted to everyone to leave their seats in the front three to four rows as there were twelve or thirteen priests coming and the seats were reserved for them. The steward told the nun to stop praying until the people had left the seats reserved for the priests.

No one moved away, later he came back again and shouted angrily, "Leave the seats now! I won't tell you again." He did this three times and still everyone was praying. Some people in the front were old and sick, but that didn't matter, they had to make room for the priests. I thought this is the same as Mother

188

Teresa's place. The priests come first. But they are fit and healthy and can stand like a lot of others. Why should people have to move to let them sit?

The steward came back again, sweat dripping from his face. He shouted, "Now come on, everyone. Move! If I have to tell you again it will be embarrassing for me and you." The people started to move out.

Then the priest came out again shouting, "Get your medals, pictures, statues or rosaries from the shop to be blessed later this afternoon."

The steward brought out electric fans; the place was very hot with all the candles burning. The man had told us on the bus journey to bring candles and flowers, that there was going to be a vision on Friday of Our Lady.

This is why the place was so packed. The local people told me it was the first time there was a traffic jam in Achill. One man stopped me in the street and asked me what was going on. When I told him he laughed and said, "The best thing to come out of Achill is the old people's home and the House of Prayer."

Back in the convent people were still praying. The steward came in again and told people to go and have lunch but come back at 2pm.

As I started to leave I saw a man in a brown jumper. I was 'told' to help him, as I walked towards him people were rushing out, not taking notice of anyone else.

The man looked bewildered; I asked him, "Are you alright? Do you want to go outside and get a seat? I'll take you."

He told me his things were behind a seat. I said, "I'll take you."

Then as he moved I noticed his white stick, the man was blind. I got his coat and hat and took him outside. Before we got to the seat Christine and the steward were coming out. I said again to her, "Can I talk with you?"

She looked at the man beside me, put her hands on his arms and started praying for him. She left again.

The man said, "What is going on?" I told him it was Christine, the visionary, praying for him.

189

"Oh, that's nice," he said. "My name is Gerry."

I sat him down, put his things under the seat and left saying, "Hope to see you again tomorrow."

I went down the road. At the bottom I was *'told'* to turn left. I did, and then I was *'told'* to go into the pub. I was surprised. I went in and had tea and sandwiches and talked to local people. I saw people that had come from other churches around Ireland, even from Belfast (Northern Ireland).

The nun must have been busy phoning around all the churches and prayer groups for this day.

A man was there with a video camera taping it all. (I wondered if it was for her tapes and if they were taping it all on a good day, when everyone was told to come).

As I came out of the pub the road was still jammed with buses and cars. The local people couldn't get over it. The crowds of people had a job to find parking spaces. As I made my way back to the House of Prayer I saw people with rosaries and other things. I asked where the shop was. They told me in the House of Prayer, just around the side. I went to look as I walked people were coming out with lots of things they had bought.

Then I started to smell India. I saw the children making all the things. As it faded I was in the shop packed with people buying everything. Some things were sold out. I couldn't believe my eyes. Most of these things I had seen being made in India under appalling conditions. I thought this is one big sham and the Catholic Church owned all the sweatshops. It is the like of these people, "so called Christian, good Catholics" that are keeping the poor children working like slaves, so that they can pray on a rosary or have a medal, statue or picture. All these things were very expensive. A woman paid £45 for one statue. One man told me he had paid £150 on medals and rosaries the day before. He said he had lots of money, he had given Christine pounds and there is a lot more to give her.

Grown men, women and children were wearing the brown scapular and they are telling people Our Lady said to wear these things. I saw them all being made in India and the Catholics are told to wear them too.

I could not move in this shop. It was packed. I was feeling so angry but I was *'told'* to just watch and not to say anything. I was *'told'* there would be children working around the clock to supply this lot and others like it until people wake up.

As I watched the shelves being emptied, yet still more people were coming in. As I was *'told'* in the visions it is just *'one big sham'*. I left the shop I had to go for a walk. I was feeling so angry. As I walked still more people were coming to the House of Prayer.

Then I saw a group of priests and nuns coming towards me. I was *'told'* to follow them. I turned round and walked behind them. One of the priests seemed angry and said he did not want to come. As they talked we got to the grounds of the House of Prayer. Prayers were being said; people were filling their bottles with so called 'holy water' and wasting so much water in between filling. As I looked at the priest I saw lovely colours around him. A man came over to the priest and told him to go inside.

"No thanks!" he said, "I'm fine right here."

So I was *'told'* – *'go inside'*.

As I made my way to the door a man helper put his arm across the door. "You cannot come in!"

"Why not?" I asked, "I was here earlier on."

"I know," he said, "now the place is full you have to stay outside."

I knew there were empty seats and something was going on. So I went around to the toilets, there was a big queue, as there were just two toilets.

People were saying the rosary.

Then I was *'told'* to keep watching. As they said the rosary with the beads people started to kiss the rosary. One woman in particular, I was watching the rosary beads enter her mouth. She was going all around it in her mouth. At some point I could not see the beads, they were all in her mouth. Then she would rub it all over her face and start kissing it again. I was *'told'* to keep watching, after a few minutes more I saw her face go all red and lots of blotches come up all around her mouth. I was *'told'* *'they can't see or hear'*.

191

I went back to the front of the convent. After a while Christine, her priest and a steward came out. Everyone gathered round and the priest talked.

Christine did see Our Lady he said and went on to tell what she had said and what it all meant. He told everyone Our Lady had blessed all that was there that day but what he said I had heard before and it was about a nun in a German prison that had seen Our Lady with blood dripping from her fingers. (It was supposed to have happened over 100 years ago. So why was this priest saying this now? (Did he look this up and prepare himself to say this today).

A group of people beside me started to laugh.

I thought they must have also heard about this. They started to walk away laughing and said, "Oh yes and the devil's not bad either!"

As I looked back at the priest talking I could see his head and shoulders looked red and the rest of him black. He also made it clear she and the House of Prayer were a symbol of the Catholic Church and their differences had been worked out.

I didn't want to hear any more. I walked away. A woman stopped me and asked what I thought of it all. She had a lovely aura so I talked to her. I said, "I think it's all a sham and that maybe Christine would be better on her own, without the priest." I said it's the same as Mother Teresa. They are jumping on her back. The women agreed with me, she also told me the nun of the House of Prayer had rang her church priest asking people to come. I also found they did this in India. I looked around to see if the good priest was still there. I spotted him sitting on the wall. I went to sit just below him with one of the men from the coach. We talked for a while then the priest and his friends got up to go, so did I. We bumped into each other. I asked him his name.

"Oh, I am not a priest," he said, "I am a brother," and told me his name.

I laughed, "You're having me on?" I said.

"No," he said with a big smile, "that is what my mam named me."

I went on to tell him of the lovely colours surrounding him and that God had *'told'* me to follow him.

"Come and tell my friends what you told me."

Just then I saw a lovely light by him and the voice said *'He is lovely'*. He asked my name and where I lived. He said, "I hope something good comes from all this."

I said, "It will!"

As he walked away he said, "I hope so," clutching my hand.

As they left I thought I would go and look for my mam and sister.

People were heading for mass at the Church to which I'm *'told'* is all going to be done up (no surprise). I found them and we decided to go in the pub. I went in earlier to have some tea. Some of my mam's friends came too and then we went for a walk. My mam and sister went to mass and I walked in with them but then out again.

Later I was *'told'* there were two collections and the plates were full of notes, cheques and coins.

I walked around the island. At one point I was *'told'* to take my shoes off and feel the earth beneath my feet. I did this looking all around at the beautiful scenery of rivers and mountains. I stood on the wooden fencing in my bare feet. I put my shoes back on and went on.

Everyone was leaving the church. I was *'told'* to go inside. There were a few people still praying the rosary. My attention was to a table at the back of the church, a book called 'Reality' there was a story in it of two young boys from Northern Ireland that were sent away years ago. Then I left.

I was *'told'* to go to the House of Prayer. I did, there were just a handful of people there now but I got this beautiful feeling (as before) as if there was someone waiting for me to give me a beautiful big hug and it felt lovely.

I was *'told'* again to sit in a seat. It was on the left, right opposite the doorway to the hall to another door to where I was standing in the morning. Then I was *'told'* bend your head put your hands to your head and face. I did this, after a while I was *'told'* to put the palms of your hands over your eyes. As I did this

I felt and saw a beautiful light. It was white then green then orange. It had a burning sensation. I looked up and saw the beautiful colours, like a haze and put my hands over my eyes. Again it went on for about fifteen to twenty minutes. It was lovely, so peaceful. I didn't want to move.

Then the silence was broken; a women's voice said to everyone, "Take the flowers and candles home. If you don't they will only be thrown out."

I couldn't believe what I was hearing. People had come and sent these lovely flowers and candles. They should be left until dead and then thrown out. But the women shouted again to people coming in, "Please take the flowers away."

I was *'told' - this is very wrong*. Then I was *'told'* look to the right, as I did Christine was coming out of her room and was leaving. I was told to see her. I went out and saw her looking out of the door.

I said "Christine can I talk to you? God took me to India to see Mother Teresa and here to see you." She looked shocked.

"Oh," she said.

I was to tell her that God was bringing down the Catholic Church and did she want to be brought down too.

But she jumped into her car, as I looked at her through the front car window she reversed it around with the steward in the back, then the priest came running out jumped in beside her and they drove off. She would not talk.

A little girl stood beside me and shouted after her, "Goodbye granny."

I said, "Is that your granny?"

"Yes," she said.

It took me back to my childhood with my gran. This little girl felt as I did - her aura dropped.

"Never mind," I said, touching her shoulder and head, "you will see her later won't you?"

"Yes," she said.

I went back into the chapel, thinking Mother Teresa knew different. She did talk. I watched people taking flowers. Some people took big candles, many of these having not been lit! I thought how sad it all was. I left, after praying and back to the bed and breakfast. It was after 10pm the lady gave us a cup of tea and biscuits.

The next day (Saturday) we would be leaving for home. As I packed my bag I was *'told'* to ask the landlady if I could fill my water bottle from her tap, it was all the same water.

Again I was *'told'* to go to the house of prayer. As I did the nun was just inside the door taking everything down. The place felt empty. As I went to walk in she said, "You can't come in this way!"

"Oh," I said, "I did yesterday."

"You go around to the other side!"

There was nothing spiritual about this nun. If such a beautiful thing happened yesterday why was the nun like this today?

I was going to tell her I was writing about it all. But again I was *'told'* to say nothing. I had seen enough. I went on my way to walk around. I went to where I took my shoes off the day before, where I was *'told'* to put my bare feet on the earth. It was lovely, as I jumped on the wooden fencing, looking out to the fields.

I asked, "Is this where I get peace now?" Straight away I was answered, *'you will get peace when you write the book'.*

I made my way back to the coach to leave. There were still a lot of people coming in on the bus. We were taking the coach around the island. Before we set off the driver told us of the famine days when people from the island went across Scotland to pick potatoes and also the graves where a lot of famine victims were buried.

As we drove around we stopped on top of a hill. The scenery was beautiful. I thought I would love to have a tent and come here to meditate and pray. One day I will. I can get everything I want from the scenery, land and God's creation but not man's buildings.

The bus driver told us if we wanted we could walk down and he would pick us up at the bottom. I walked and so did a few others. The road felt soft beneath my feet. I felt alive spiritually. I learnt more by coming here and had had my eyes opened a bit wider. On the bus back home everyone was talking about the event. Then the women in front of me started talking to me. I was sitting alone, and then she took some flowers from her bag and was giving them to me. Flowers and water I will always accept, but these flowers had sadness around them and I could not accept them, besides, the *'voice'* was telling me not take them.

The women from Dublin looked at me, "They are alright," she said, "I had them from the house of prayer, the sister said we could all take them or they would be thrown away."

"Yes I know they did, a lady told us the same."

I thanked her but said I couldn't accept them.

"Alright," she said and got her rosary beads out to pray.

I couldn't help wondering where these beads had been made and of the suffering. Did any of these people in the coach ever think of this?

As we were coming into Arklow over the bridge it was midnight. The place was packed and the town was closed off. There was a big firework display. The coach had to go around left by the river and down the fishery, letting people off as we go.

One man said he hoped he would be up for mass next Sunday morning. With that the man behind me said, "The priest there blesses the tap only," (which is a good idea, as all the water comes out of it).

I said, "He is only a man, he can't bless water."

"No," He said.

"God gave us all the same power. It's up to us if we use it or not. We are all the same," I said. I think he is still looking at me but at least I gave him something to think about.

I was *'told'* about eating out one day and that I was to go to Glendalough.

Having no car to do this I looked up the buses and coaches travelling there. All I knew was that I was to go there before I went back to Cornwall, England.

My family had arranged for us all to go to dinner the Sunday before I left. I know I would not be going but I did not know why. Then down with my brother one day he said, "Do you want to go to Glendalough on Sunday?"

I couldn't believe it. "Yes," I said quickly, "that's if the weather is good!"

Sunday came and off we went. He told me to drive, as my sister had leant us the car for the day. The sun was shining and it was a lovely day. I knew it would be.

We got there early, talking and laughing along the way. As we went walking around Glendalough we saw a group of visitors with a guide telling them all about the monks that lived here from the 6th century and what they did. I was 'told' to join the group.

I said, "Come on," to my brother and off we went (you learn so much from a guide).

We got to a huge Celtic cross. He told us this was the oldest cross in Ireland, as far as he knew. With that I saw ivy and grass growing up all over this cross. I could not believe it. This was the cross I had seen in my visions. I never knew what it meant. I also saw the visions in my church when I used to go to mass. Ivy and grass were growing all around and up it (the oldest cross). Then I heard the guide's voice again.

"Now," he said, "this is the end of the tour but there are lakes here, the upper and lower lake." He gave us directions on how to get there. My brother said I have heard of the upper lake but have never been there before.

I was 'told' to go there. We got to the lower lake. It was beautiful. I remembered coming to Glendalough when I was about 14-15 to see St Kevin's bed here. It was a big stone rock.

We sat for a while then we made our way up to the upper lake. As we got there, there were children playing in the water. Lots of people were around, all of different nationalities. We sat for a while. I was 'told' to go and walk into the water. I went forward, took my sandals off and went to walk in the water. It was so cold! As I looked around at the beautiful view I saw a small child in the water he came rushing out of this water. He said, "It's so cold!" as he went past me, splashing water all over my long dress.

197

I had seen all this in a vision weeks before but I didn't know where it was and I didn't have a dress that colour 'red' like terracotta. Yet in the vision I remember the dress and the little boy splashing me. All I was thinking was 'my new dress!'

We were invited to a wedding and I had only just bought this dress a few days before I went to Ireland. I was a bit bent up at the cold water. Then I 'heard' - *stand to the circle*. I thought 'what circle?' then my body started to straighten up. As I looked up the lake there was a blazing light, 1,000 times brighter than the sun pure white light. It was moving towards me, getting bigger and bigger. I was told to take two steps further in. As I did this the water and earth beneath my feet were so hot. Then I was *'told'* – *'look to the circle'*, as I did this I couldn't believe I wasn't afraid. It became like silver, then gold. It was pulsating, moving nearer to me. I felt wonderful. Then beautiful colours came shooting from it, then back to white, silver white and gold. It was so big. Then I was *'told'* – *'Look for the truth in your circle of life. 'Look for truth in the circle of life'*.

It started to fade. I looked around and wondered if anyone else had seen anything. I looked at my brother; he had taken photos of me in the water, children playing. I didn't want to move, it was such a lovely feeling. I stayed in the water for a while thinking about what had happened. It had been so beautiful and I wasn't afraid anymore.

As we made our way back to the lower lake and back to the car my brother said he was glad he had seen the two lakes. So was I.

Notes
The picture at the front of the chapter is of Achill Island.

Chapter 18

Reflection

That's the beauty of it all, you never know what a day will bring,' I was *'told'.* True religion is a simple faith, no need for a church, temple, mosque, synagogue, doctrine or dogma of any kind. Our own Self is all of the above. We need peace, truth, justice and above all … freedom. We are born free, nothing attached to us, and then we are labelled with what our parents or guardians want. We are moulded into society.

We learn to hate each other rather than love. The Catholic Church teachings all those outside Catholics were going to hell. I remember the nuns teaching us 'would we stand up for our religion?' and we would shout back "yes!"

"Will you fight for your religion?" and we would all shout back "yes!"

We were told not to speak to the Protestants. The Protestant school was beside our school. Children going past it in the morning would shout: "Proddy, proddy on the wall, half a loaf would do you all." Yet I could see they were just like us, no different at all. We were told not to go to pagan churches or take part in anything they do. I remember a priest saying in church at mass, if anyone had to go to pagan England to work they were not to go with any other religion but their own. If they got asked to a protestant wedding and could not get out of going they must not take part in any service. Just sit throughout the ceremony. I was being told what he is saying is not right.

I remember my friends Mary, Alice, Ann and myself going up to the top of the town to see the Protestant church. It looked big, with lovely grounds and black railings around it. We felt brave that day. We wanted to go inside, to see what it was like. As we made our way up to the big doors I was hoping they would be locked, but they were open. As we looked around making sure no one saw us - in we went. As we were looking around we found ourselves near the front of the alter, when we all saw it at the same time - this big bird with a book on it. We thought it was the devil. We ran for our lives, with my friend Alice falling down. Mary and I were so afraid to go and help her. She shouted after us, we ran back got her up and ran like hell, we were so frightened!

We never told anyone what we had done and we never went back again. This fear was put into us. We were not born with it.

One day we went around in the car to see the Red Cross on the way to Avoca. As we were coming into Avoca, I was driving. My brother was beside me with his shirt off and sun shining. We stopped down a narrow lane. A man was passing us, pushing his bike up the hill.

He said, "Hello," and looked at my brother, "by Jesus you look queer and being driven around as well!"

We laughed and my brother said to him, "That's a fine cigar you have in your hand there!" The cigar was so big; we laughed as we entered Avoca and had a drink in a local pub there.

We talked to some visitors and went around the shops and here again I saw things being sold that had been made in India. I told the girls in the shop this and left.

We went on to The Meeting of the Waters, Tom Moors Tree and The Vale of Avoca. Here I was told to put my feet into the water in between where the two rivers meet. I did this and it felt warm and nice. My brother took photos of the views. I was *'told'* – '*look to the front, stand straight then turn clockwise around'*. I did this then after a while I sat down on the steps behind me. I felt so warm.

When I had talked about all these bad things and had written to everyone including the Church and my MP I felt worn out and tired.

What else could I do? Everyone was passing the buck. No one got back to me saying they were doing something about it, not even to see if I was ok. Everyone wanted it kept quiet or else no one would give any money.

"Do not rock the boat," the Church had told me. "I had undone a can of worms that maybe would have been better left shut."

As I was sitting down one day I was thinking what am I going to do now. Then I was taken forward as if I was moving at speed. I was standing in a beautiful valley with trees, hills and a stream about 5-6ft wide in front of me. I was *'told'* – *'look across'*. As I did I saw a beautiful white glowing mist in front of me. As the mist lifted there was an Indian man dressed in a black and white top with black trousers standing opposite me on the other side of the stream. He bowed his head to me with a slight smile on his face, he had two feathers at the back of his head. The left one was slightly bent. I was *'told'* – *'his name is Joseph'*, then *'Chief Joseph'*. It was so peaceful here I thought. With that I was moving again at speed and then sitting in my home.

So I went to find out about Chief Joseph. I went to the library and was told which book to look for. As I read about this man one thing he said, "Here, my chiefs I am tired. My heart is

201

sick and sad from where the sun stands I will fight no more forever."

As I read this I thought (this is how I felt). Then in front of me again I saw Joseph. I was *'told'* he was my past life. I heard again, *'When the missionaries came we had land now they have the land and we have the prayer books'*.

When I came back from touring Ireland I was asked to my friends son's wedding. It was a Catholic church. I didn't really want to go as I didn't believe in any of it anymore and of the way they are carrying on in India.

I thought of it for a long time then I thought I can't let that get in the way but then I was *'told'* I was to go. The time came and we travelled up country for the wedding day. We set off for the church.

We went into a pub to have a drink. As I looked across I *'saw'* a lovely aura around the fields and in front of us, then I saw stones. I said to my friend, "Is that the stones? They look like Stonehenge."

"Yes," she said.

I never knew about this place but Ann had seen it before.

Jo said, "I'm taking you in there after your drink."

I felt so excited and the warmth I felt as I entered the gate was beautiful. The whole area had warmth about it. This was the day before the wedding. I was so surprised to see Avebury and the corn crops. I never knew about this place and was shocked to see all the colours on the top of the stones as we entered Avebury. The colours on the stones were the very same colours I saw in Ireland at New Grange.

This was the first time I saw the church, as all the family were busy taking photos. I was told to go into the church. I was surprised; as I was looking around this church I was *'told'* go in and look around. As I did there was another alter and seats. A lady was sitting down; another going around to see everything was ok.

Then the lady turned around and said, "Hello."

"Oh," I said, "you're Irish." As she spoke we talked about Ireland and she told me this side is the old church and in there is the new church. I don't know how it happened but we talked about the Church priests and what was coming out about the sexual and physical abuse.

Then she said, "You don't want to worry about all that. A lot of that is not true, our monsignor told us last Sunday from the alter there would be a lot of things coming out about the Church but not to believe them all. God and the 'Blessed Lady' will sort it all out."

I said, "Did you know about the sweat shops?" I went on to tell her what I found in India. "I'm like you and believe me; I'm telling you the truth."

"Oh dear," she said and again, "don't worry God will sort it out."

With that I was 'told' – 'look behind', as I did the other woman had a pole, she pulled down the silver dome putting out the candle, with her other hand she pulled out the old candle put another one in and lit it up again.

I could not believe it! She had pulled the candle down and pushed it up with no thought at all. I went back to my childhood. The nuns and priests telling us if the light is out then you know God is not there. He is angry with you and not in the Church, make sure every time you come into the Church you look for the light.

(And do you know - I always did! Even at my age now). Seeing this took the wind out of my sales, we had been fools.

Then I heard my name - they were calling me. My friend was there with a big smile on her face. I had come to the wedding saying I would not say anything. I would keep my mouth shut. Oh God, I cannot tell her, not now anyway.

We went in and sat down. Then I saw the priest enter, he did not look or sound nice, but I didn't say anything. As he was taking Holy Communion when most people bow their heads I was 'told' to keep looking at him. He went to put the Holy Communion in his mouth it turned into the shape of an arrow as he put it into his mouth. I could see it going down his throat and then it stuck. I could see it all. He drank all his wine but it still didn't move, it frightened him and he ran off quickly to the other alter and came back with more wine and drank it all down, but it didn't go down.

Later everyone was saying, "What was he doing?"

Then I told them, "The communion had got stuck in his throat."

"Oh, is that what it was," they said, still taking photos outside.

The priest was also now outside, talking to the car driver. Then I was moving fast again and I was '*shown*' the same church in bad repair, weeds growing everywhere, the door falling off and open. A rat sat on his two hind legs at the steps of the door looking in.

I was '*told*' in the vision in the future it will be like this and even a rat won't go inside. Then I was back again the priest was still talking to the driver.

Next we went to the hotel for a meal. We were talking in a group and one Irish lady heard my accent.

"Oh," she said, "they are talking about our monsignor but *he* changes his voice to speak louder, they don't know our monsignor." Then I was '*told*' – '*neither does she*'.

I thought afterwards (God is dealing with them) - Then in a vision I was '*told*' - '*put it all in a book for me*'. I thought (I can't do that). I have met some lovely nuns, some good brothers and priests who didn't like what was going on. I was '*told*' I wasn't to worry about that; '*a good nun, priest, brother or person will have nothing to worry about. No one will come knocking on their door*'.

On Sunday 22 September 2000 it was time to come home on the coach. Halfway home there was an accident. The coach was going slowly. I was '*told*' to look to the person across from me to my left. I was looking out of the window, as we got to the accident the woman looking out of the window wearing dark glasses shouted, "Oh!" and shook, she looked away and brought her hands to cover her eyes.

There was a dark cloud around her as she did this and then she pushed it over her eyes. I was '*told*' – '*She would have been better to look and if one couldn't help then to see it and hope everything would be all right. Not to shut a thing out. It's only by seeing and hearing that we can do things and change things and ourselves*'.

Then further on, right in front of me was like a huge cinema screen. I saw myself at the wedding with all the people and it went right back through my life, then it stopped. I was shown myself in India, from the last time I went there and all the people I had helped like all the orphans. It went right through me and then stopped.

Then I was asked, "What road do you want to take?" Still looking at myself at the wedding and then the other side of me in India I had already answered the question in my head and I couldn't wait to say 'the Indian road'.

With that it all faded. I was shocked but delighted. I looked around and wondered if anyone had seen anything. There were many changes ahead.

I was *'told'* – *'We are all going to remember more of our birth visions and reincarnations. We will be guided individually, our intuition and consciousness will take us to where we need to go and who to see and be with. We need to act now, before we leave this body and see our whole life in front of us. Don't leave it until it is too late - act now. Do your bit for the planet.'*

As I was *'told'* I'm not responsible for people's reactions to what I have told them. I am only responsible for what I was taken to India to *'see'* and *'hear'* and to talk and write about it.

We own nothing, we came with nothing and we go with nothing. The land belongs to no one; it will be here until we destroy it. We come to learn truths. What we do is up to us. But each and every one of us has to answer for our actions or inactions no matter what colour, religion or status we are. We need to learn more of where we came from and where we go to.

I remember sitting and talking to Mother Teresa in her convent in September 1994 and a woman coming to visit and talk with her. She was between fifty-five and sixty. She was covered in thick gold jewellery around her neck, arms and fingers. The smell of perfume from her made me cough. My eyes began to water. I said to Mother Teresa I would have to go, I couldn't stand the smell of perfumes or anything similar, they made me feel bad and sick. To my amazement she told me she felt the same.

(No doubt the woman's perfume cost a lot of money). As I looked at her body it was getting darker. I could hardly see her, only the gold stood out. Then I was *'told'* – *'that was most important to her'*.

On leaving India a priest gave me the name and address of a diplomat. I was told I could give him any amount of money or send anything, as they are never checked!

On the 1st January 2000 I was shown a big, old tree. Images appeared on the tree like the below:

Masked man with gun

Sphinx	**Pharaoh**
Young Black Bird	**Black Child**
Peacock's Feather	**White Butterfly**
Eye	**Owl**
Robin	

I was travelling fast again. I was *'told'* the time was 10th – 12th Century, 12th – 14th Century in Africa fighting tribes. I was standing watching a dark man being hanged by his long curly hair to a tree. Under his bare feet was a fire. It had been burning for a long time. I watched as the men went off into the bushes. A little later another man appeared. I know him I thought. He had a flat metal knife, which he used to cut across the hair of the man hanging. He carried him off in his arms. The man hanging, I was told, was me. I watched as the other man put leaves on his

206

feet, cover them with sackcloth and tie it with banana leaves to help heal the feet.

Then I was moving fast again. I was *told* this is Cornwall, lots of black smoke and mist over a field. I was fighting against the crown - lots of men in fields. Then I saw a trench three men had just dug. They looked so young I could feel their fear. As the last man jumped in I was *'told'* it was me.

It was like I could feel myself jumping into the trench.

One day I was *'told'* to look out the window, as I did I suddenly saw two birds flying - one black, one white. The black was fighting to stay up as it struggled for a while. Then I saw it falling, and then the whole scene disappeared.

I have knocked on so many doors about all this. I may as well have knocked my head against a wall.

This book is not just for me it is also for the millions of people the religions and governments have hurt and treated unjustly over the years and is still hurting today. It's for people who haven't been able or won't talk. I'm that voice and now it's up to you to be that voice too.

Notes

The picture at the front of the chapter is of a candle in an oil burner.

Poetry

To Give

To give to people where it is needed
This is what it should be about

To walk up to a mud hut and give
To walk to a house - give, turn and walk away
To walk to a tent in a field
where just a candle flickers at night
To give and walk away

To throw money from a passing train
to people in the fields
To give to people in the street
To go into a village where they have nothing
To give and walk away, no questions asked
To give to a child washing his sores
in a mud rainy stream
To touch his head
See the smile on his surprised face
To touch each other with just a smile says it all
To give to a child brushing his teeth
To give to a child cleaning and brushing the train
To give to someone selling you something at a
station
when the train stops and you take nothing.
See the big open eyes
See the beauty in the face

The Traveller

The Elements

A true leader does not only care about his flock and to hell with the rest of the world. A true leader cares about the whole world and then some.

The Traveller

Me

I am only me
I can't change the world on my own
I need help from you
But I can change the world for some people
With your help we can change it for a lot more,
more and more
Don't let us stop trying
For the good of us and our planet

The Traveller

***

Making the Headlines

The following short unedited extracts of stories are from popular newspapers. These articles back up many of the first-hand experiences witnessed by the author or eyewitness accounts from contacts made in India.

West Country News
Wednesday 17 September 1997
Probe into misuse of India's £65m aid cash
A government inquiry was launched last night to find out why £65 million of tax payers' money earmarked for humanitarian aid in India was misused to buy helicopters made in the West country...
by David Cracknell

Irish Mirror
Tuesday 22 July 1997
Depraved beyond belief – Pervert priest's victims tell of appalling abuse.
The 70 year old sex monster, pictured left, yesterday, pleaded guilty to 74 charges of abuse against 13 girls and 7 boys.
 All his victims were under 15 when he assaulted them. One was just six...
By Neil Leslie

The Sunday Times Magazine
Sunday 2 May 1999
Twisted Sisters
Many Irish woman had their lives ruined by children's homes, where they were beaten, humiliated and abused. But because their tormentors were often nuns, their stories have remained strictly taboo. Now they are asking for confessions.
Peter and Leni Gillman investigate...

Mirror Magazine
Tuesday 18 January 2000
God's child prostitutes
They're forced to have sex with any man who wants them, shunned by everyone in their village and destined for a life of poverty and abuse. *Brigid McConville* meets the forgotten victims of India's cruellest religious tradition.
"I was pregnant at the age of 12. The men treated us as slaves for sex and work.
Policemen came into the village to rape us"

Daily Mail
Tuesday 17 March 1998
Exposed, the child sponsorship 'myth'
Charities that offer donors the chance to sponsor impoverished children overseas may not provide the individual help expected, an investigation suggests.
Daily Mail writer

Sunday Independent
Sunday 29 March 1998
Christian Brothers say sorry to abuse victims
A religious order which has taught an estimated half a million Irish children has apologised for the hurt suffered by anyone abused in its care.
By Charles Mallon

The Express
Wednesday 3 June 1998
So cheated in life, but so proud in death.
For six days, Wol Diing Ajek led his starving family across the wastelands of Sudan. Three of his four children died on the hellish journey and then, as he reached safety, this brave man finally gave up his life.
By Ros Wynne –Jones

211

When a poor person dies of hunger, it has not happened because God did not take care of him or her. It has happened because neither you nor I wanted to give that person what he or she needed."

Mother Teresa

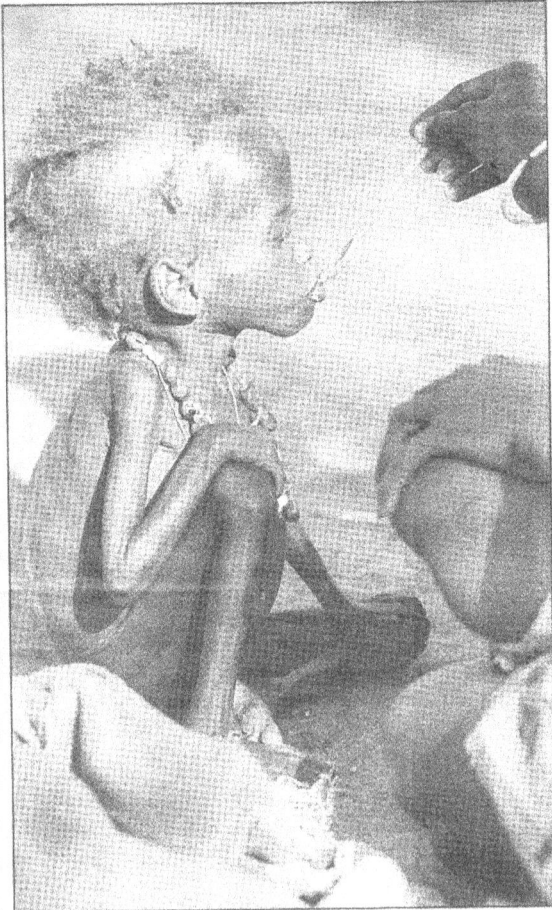

Photo by Michael Dunlea

This is the world's shame (it's up to you!)

The Times
Tuesday 31 March 1998
Orphans 'tortured and beaten by nuns in Australia'
Hundreds of orphaned children, many from Britain, suffered public floggings, sadistic torture and sexual abuse at the hands of Roman Catholic nuns, an Australian academic said yesterday...

By Roger Maynard in Sydney and our foreign staff.

Sunday Mirror
Sunday 7 June 1998
Scandal of the children cruelly dumped 12,000 miles from home
I thought it was a day trip but they were sending me off to Australia.
When my own mother came to the convent in Middlesborough for me, 10 years before I was sent away, she was told I was adopted. It was as deceitful as the way the nuns changed my name. I was born Elizabeth but they brought me up to believe my real name was Pamela.
"They told me that nothing was known about my background or where I came from - a terrible lie that would haunt me for decades."
By Anthea Gerrie

The Mirror
Thursday 16 July 1998
Priest is jailed after sexually abusing boys.
Perverts assaults began in the 1970's.
A pervert priest who sexually abused two young boys was yesterday jailed for seven-and-a-half years at Dublin's Circuit Criminal Court...
By Cormac MacRuairi

The Irish Times
Monday 17 July 1997
Parents call for Enquiry into 3-in-1 vaccination damage.
Claim that children were used in trials on vaccine in Dublin
orphanages in 1970's.
Hundreds of Irish families are struggling with children brain
damaged as a result of the three-in-one vaccine, and a number
are considering legal action for compensation, according to a
woman whose son was awarded £2.75 million in the high court
in 1993...
By Alison O'Connor

Sunday Mirror
Sunday 3 October 1999
Balls make £10m - slaves get 10p
Official match balls of the rugby World Cup are being made
by children as young as 10 in horrific sweat shops...
By Graham Johnson in the Punjab, India

Sunday Mirror
Sunday 27 June 1999
10p a day NHS slaves
Scandal of children aged 8 who toil 13 hours a day in
sweatshops to make instruments for hospitals. And their boss
says, 'It keeps them off the streets'.
Their bodies are deformed by working 13 hours a day in
cramped, sweltering workshops. They risk death or loss of
limb as they operate machines. They face being blinded by
metal sparks flying through the air. These are the children -
some as young as 8 - who earn a mere 10p a day for their
slave labour in Pakistan.
But there is an even more disturbing side to their grim
existence. The surgical instruments they craft for a pittance are
destined for NHS hospitals across Britain...
By Graham Johnson In Pakistan and Tim Mies

Evening Herald (Ireland's Evening Newspaper)
Wednesday 21 March 2001(Front Page – Edited extract
below:)
Mystery: Church says no rape allegations against Irish
Priests here or abroad. SEX CLAIM NUN GOES TO
GROUND.

Sister Maura compiled shocking evidence in her 1195 report to the Vatican that Catholic clerics are using their positions to gain sexual favours from nuns in 23 countries. The countries listed in her report are Botswana, Burundi, Brazil, Columbia, Ghana, India, Ireland, Italy, Kenya, Lesotho, Malawi, Nigeria, Papua New Guinea, Philippines, South Africa, Sierra Leone, Tanzania, Tonga, Uganda, United States, Zambia, Zaire and Zimbabwe…

… The Vatican spokesman, Dr Joaquin Navarro-Valls, yesterday acknowledged that the "problem is known about" but it insisted that it was "restricted" to a geographical area, understood to mean Africa
By Fiona Dillon

Let's Do it Now!

Hello everyone.

As most of you know I have travelled through India now for eleven years, I don't have to tell you of the poverty in places there.   You have all seen Africa and Live Aid, the same thing is happening in India and other places in the world. I am not a charity, nor am I with the church so every penny I get goes to the people. What they want and *need*, from a jeep, van and cows to rice hospital bills, water pumps, an operation for a little girl, pay for children to go to school and the saddest of all, to buy children out of slavery (bond) and put them back with their families. But I just want you to think for a moment, where have all your things come from, who made them all? I saw everything we use being made in India, all we eat too, fruit, spices, vegetables, pepper, rice, etc. to everything we have in the home, in the garden, in the churches, down to the blocks to build. Did they have a FAIR DEAL – NO – NO – NO (not what I saw!)

But now 'we' can change the map, think before you give money, make sure you know where it is going, to help with one hand could bring blood on the other hand.

We can change the map, *LET'S DO IT NOW!*

The Traveller

'I live, eat and sleep with the people'
From Hand to Hand – 100%

Letters

The following are letters of reply sent to The Traveller from letters she had sent to the people and organisations on issues of great concern she had found in India and already outlined in this book.

I WILL TAKE YOU THROUGH THE STARS

Rome,
Italy

May, 2005

His Holiness Pope Benedict XVI
The Vatican,
Rome,
Italy

Dear Pope Benedict XVI,

I wish you well in your new role. I also wish that you would look into the activities of your Church members abroad. In the course of my charity work I have travelled throughout India and have spoken to many who have travelled in other poor countries. I have witnessed or have been made aware of atrocities perpetrated by members of the Catholic Church, such as bishops, priests, brothers, and some nuns. These include: Abuse, sexual abuse, and beatings; slavery (Bond) within the houses of bishops and priests; experiments on orphan children and adults in Catholic Institutions; young girls put to marry old men; babies taken from young girls who were made pregnant by bishops, priests, or brothers, and then adopted out to the public – I saw nuns similarly made pregnant, and some even too afraid for their lives to say anything. I have been told that such things have been going on for a long time, and that no one does anything to help the victims or to get it stopped. The Church has taken so much land away from the poor people that they can no longer afford to look after their families, and some cannot subsist. In 1996 your Church accumulated so much land from the people of India that it shocked some people within the Church. I saw children working from dawn to dusk in catholic sweatshops, for little or no money. I saw young men walking like zombies, afraid to look right or left, their spirits broken working within priests' houses. All this I saw first hand, and I must say that I was ashamed to call myself a catholic. I have heard it said that you are God's people, but I don't think so.

I end with the hope and prayer that, in the name of God, you will have these things looked into, that you will have such malpractice eradicated during your papacy, and that you will do something to help the unfortunate people affected.

Yours sincerely,

The Traveller

MATTHEW TAYLOR MP

HOUSE OF COMMONS
LONDON SW1A 0AA

10th September 1997

Please quote ref:566/97/mt/gld
Your ref:

Dear Traveller

Many thanks indeed for getting in touch with me at my recent
travelling surgery.

To be honest it is hard to know what an MP could do about the
particular allegations you have - they are really for the church
(though you might contact the Media).

In view of Mother Teresa's recent death however, you may feel that
this is not the right time to take it forward.

Yours sincerely

I WILL TAKE YOU THROUGH THE STARS

Matthew Taylor MP

HOUSE OF COMMONS
LONDON SW1A 0AA

08/10/01   Please quote ref:836/01/mt/dhw

Dear Traveller

~~Many thanks indeed for coming to see me at my recent travelling surgery.~~

I am sorry to hear about your continuing concerns about the Catholic Church, especially its operations in India. These are difficult for me to pursue as a Member of Parliament, as they are really matters for the Church or the Indian authorities.

Indeed, from what you said you have been pursuing this with the Church, with some success.

Thank you, however, for letting me know of your continuing efforts.

Yours sincerely

Foreign &
Commonwealth
Office
King Charles Street
London
SW1A 2AL

7 January 2003

Dear **Traveller**

Thank you for your letter dated 10 October to HM The Queen about drug trials in India. I have been asked to respond as a member of the staff at the Foreign Office dealing with our relations with the region.

We have made enquiries through our High Commission in India regarding this issue. They are not aware of any specific allegations of this sort. In order to make further enquiries they would need to have more information.

India has a robust parliamentary tradition, an independent judiciary, professional and apolitical armed forces, a vibrant civil society, and free and outspoken media. India has signed and ratified all of the six core UN human rights treaties except the Convention Against Torture (CAT), which it has signed but not ratified. We continue to encourage India to ratify CAT. But Indian performance against the fundamental rights covered by these Covenants is patchy and well documented. Implementation varies from state to state and awareness of human rights issues is inconsistent. As a result, women, children, minorities, Scheduled Castes and Scheduled Tribes often suffer violations of their human rights. The socially and economically disadvantaged sections of society are particularly vulnerable. Mike O'Brien most recently discussed a wide range of human rights issues with the Government of India on 17 October, during his visit to the region.

Yours sincerely

Miss J Baldwin
South Asia Department

221

Foreign &
Commonwealth
Office
King Charles Street
London
SW1A 2AL

26 February 2003

Dear **Traveller**

Thank you for your letter dated 22 January about drug trials in India.

As I mentioned in my letter of 7 January, we made enquiries through our High Commission in India regarding this issue. I have again asked them if there has been any reports and without any further information we are unable to take our enquiries further.

Yours sincerely

Miss J Baldwin
South Asia Department

BUCKINGHAM PALACE

11th October, 2002.

Dear **Traveller**

The Queen has asked me to thank you for your letter of 10th October expressing your concern that people in India have taken part in drug testing for various diseases. Her Majesty has taken careful note of your comments.

As a constitutional Sovereign, The Queen acts on the advice of her Ministers, and I have, therefore, been instructed to send your letter to the Right Honourable Jack Straw MP, the Secretary of State for Foreign and Commonwealth Affairs, so that he may know of your approach to Her Majesty on this matter, and may consider the points you raise.

Yours sincerely,

Mrs. Deborah Bean
Chief Correspondence Officer

I WILL TAKE YOU THROUGH THE STARS

ST. JAMES'S PALACE
LONDON SW1A 1BS

From: The Office of HRH The Prince of Wales

18th October, 2002

Dear **Traveller**

The Prince of Wales has asked me to thank you for your letter of 10th October in connection with your acute concern for the well-being of orphaned children in India who you say are being used in drug trials.

Your reasons for writing as you did are appreciated and His Royal Highness is grateful to you for bringing this very serious matter to his attention.

I am aware that you have written to Her Majesty The Queen on this subject and that her office have brought this matter to the attention of The Foreign Secretary, The Rt. Hon. Jack Straw MP.

The Prince of Wales has asked me to send you his best wishes.

Yours sincerely,

Mrs. Claudia Holloway

This is the first book written by 'The Traveller'. It is about her adventures through life.

It will make you look deeply within yourself and your own experience of life as you compare yours with hers.

It may open your eyes and ears to things you never knew existed in our world, not just the supernatural but also the extent of the utter poverty and deprivation of peoples and races by the oppression of the rich and powerful.

With over ¾ of our world in utter poverty, starving to death (United Nation figures) and ¼ of the world with ¾ of the world's resources it is time for humanity to wake up from greed and complacency.

It is time for each and every one of us to make a stand – for SHARING to take the place of greed and complacency.

This book will bring the reader face to face with themselves.

Editor

This book is not just for me it is also for the millions of people the Church and governments have hurt and treated unjustly over the years and are still hurting today. It's for people who haven't been able or won't talk. I'm that voice and now it's up to you to be that voice too.

The Traveller

Index